The Zen Koan
as a means of
Attaining Enlightenment

The Zen Koan

as a means of

Attaining Enlightenment

by Daisetz Teitaro Suzuki

Charles E. Tuttle Co., Inc.
Boston • Rutland, Vermont • Tokyo

This edition first published in the United States in 1994 by
Charles E. Tuttle Co., Inc. of Rutland, Vermont and Tokyo, Japan,
with editorial offices at 153 Milk Street, Boston, Massachusetts 02109

This work was originally published by Rider & Company
in 1950, in *Essays in Zen Buddhism,* second series,
edited by Christmas Humphreys.

Introduction © 1994 Janwillem van de Wetering

ISBN 0–8048–3041–X
Library of Congress Cataloging-in-Publication data is available for this title.

Cover design by Joel Friedlander
Illustration: *Meditation Posture* (detail) by Zenchu Sato

1 3 5 7 9 10 8 6 4 2

Printed in the United States
(Mc&G)

Introduction
by Janwillem van de Wetering

This is one of the main books that got us, Zennies, all started, this is one of the Model-A Fords of Western Ch'an Buddhism.

(Sanskrit Dyana = Chinese Ch'an = Japanese Zen = regular meditation)

An age ago, in a former existence, many dreams back now, I came across this splendid vehicle at Foyles, Charing Cross Road, London, a bookstore spread through five multi-storied houses. There was an old man in the philosophy basement, a sage in suspenders, who watched my dismal perusal of Hume, Jaspers and Heidegger. The salesman/sage wanted to know what the young gent was after.

I said I wanted to know why life is a pain.

Why would the young gent want to know why life is a pain?

Why, to put an end to the pain, you old codger.

That was the right attitude, the old codger said, and sold me a D.T. Suzuki.

Delirium Tremens Who?

That was right, the old codger said. All Zen sages are out of their minds, but the actual name was Daisetz Teitaro.

Daisetz Teitaro Suzuki, I made a mantra out of the sounds and danced to them in my room at Hammersmith Terrace, with a view of the Thames, then still muddy.

The Thames got cleaned up since then.

And so did I, some, maybe, it seems. And countless other I's.

If so—thanks to Suzuki.

How does one clean up the I? By doing away with the I.

By seeing through the sucker.

There are koans to that effect, as Dr. Suzuki points out in this textbook.

Read a koan, the salesman/sage told me. Go on, open the book, pick any koan.

Gent: I worry.
Codger: Show me this I that worries.
Gent: I can't find it.
Codger: See?

I laughed. This was fun, better than the hairsplitting of analytical philosophy that redefines life=pain, after a long academic merry-go-round, a degree or two, a career, birth-middlelife crisis-death, into life=pain without ever showing a way out, except by suicide maybe.

But does suicide put an end to life=pain?

Doesn't suicide rather lead to more suffering in the bardos, after-earth limbos where we still carry names, identities, worrying I's?

What else can the astral spheres be than more pseudo-substantial hells where we are still looking for the light, while we are the light?

Heed Allen Ginsberg who sang, squeezing his harmonium May 1994: *die when you die.*

Codger Ginsberg sang through the Sony speakers, all over Sheep Meadow, (Central Park, Manhattan, New York, USA, World, Just Another Universe, Void) that we should die when we die.

No kidding. Let our I's die.

"But," Sariputra asks, "how to do that?"

We all know it now, there are five million Buddhists in the western world, cracking their koans.

(What's a koan again? A 'public case.' A case, a non-intellectual public—nothing exclusive here—riddle that anyone solves instantly, when the time is there.)

The year was 1958 when Suzuki's book found me. I was reading existentialism at University College but the despair of western egocentric doomthought depresses.

Sartre (I read) says: "We are condemned to freedom."

But surely that can't be right. Why should freedom be a burden, and if it is, shouldn't we throw it away?

"How to throw away burdensome thinking of make-believe-freedom?" asks Sariputra.

"Read me first" the Suzuki book says.

Eat me (like Alice in wonderland eating the pills: they made her grow with joy and learning, they made her shrink with joy and insight, prepared her for the Caterpillar: "WHO, ALICE, ARE *YOU*?" Then made her waft away into the Cheshire Cat's smile).

This magic box of wonderpills: Suzuki's famous essay on koan study, now in your hands, wafted down into mine.

Here was my first Zen book telling how sages make monkeys out of disciples, then set the monkeys free. How? You will see that when you plow (vintage Suzuki ain't easy reading, there is a culture difference to start off with) through this standard work on the art of releasing nothingness into the void.

Instant self-help?

Not quite, perhaps.

Although it could be, of course.

Isn't the right time now?

When I entered Daitoku-ji monastery, Kyoto, Japan, clutching Suzuki in my right armpit I asked the one and only English speaking monk how long koan study takes.

He said he was the Buddha's ape, what did he know?, but that sixteen years sounded like just about right.

There are some 1700 koans, this doorman to wisdom explained, but a lot of them are copies or variations and you can squeeze the program into a mere hundred, with three big ones up front. Once, he let me know right there and then, once you answer the big ones, the little ones fall in place easily. So—give and take a bit of time for genius or abysmal ignorance—sixteen years is about the right time span. (I would be a roshi in my forties.)

Then, when I had enough Japanese, I asked the monastic teacher, and he laughed.

Zen teachers laugh a lot, especially during sanzen.

You can, in their private quarters, (at 3:30 a.m.) ask them what's so funny and they will tell you, in their own fine way.

I was already there, the Zen teacher laughed. I had always been there. There was nothing to obstruct me. Did I know the Heart Sutra? No? He would sing it for me.

Sariputra, form is not other than emptiness
and emptiness is not other than form
form is precisely emptiness, and emptiness precisely form.

Who is Sariputra? I asked.

Sariputra was sent back to the Zendo, to more form, to more pain, more autumn flies dying heavily on my clasped hands, more smoldering of leg joints, more sadistic arrogance stupidly staged by stick-bearing holyboly office holders.

Sariputra is the Bodhisattva who starts off learning by reading books by D.T. Suzuki.

I actually met Dr. Suzuki in Japan, or he met me, or, rather, he looked at me. Ruth Fuller Sasaki, and American Zen priest, restored Ryosen-an temple and added a Zendo, gift of her First American Zen Institute to the Daitoku-ji compound. The Zendo got filled up with foreign dogs, sycophants and monkeys. I sat and suffered—suddenly the doors flung open, the venerable Mrs. Sasaki, outside, beamed, the Zen scholar Suzuki, outside, raised tufted Zen master eyebrows.

Us monkeys, inside, blinked.

"Look what I've done, D.T."

"Well done, R."

Well done indeed. Build Zendos, write books, chant the meditation-rock sutra in Central Park, compose an introduction, all to find the way out.

And thanks to Daisetz Teitaro Suzuki for pointing.

Surry, Maine, May 1994

The Zen Koan
as a means of
Attaining Enlightenment

THE KOAN EXERCISE

AS THE MEANS FOR REALIZING SATORI OR ATTAINING ENLIGHTENMENT

PART I

1. *An Experience Beyond Knowledge*

In the First Series of my *Zen Essays* (p. 331 *f.*) I have promised the reader in the Second Series to discuss fully the subject of 'koan'.[1] In fact, the koan system has effected a special development in Zen Buddhism, and is a unique contribution Zen has made to the history of the religious consciousness. When the importance of the koan is understood, we may say that more than the half of Zen is understood.

The Zen masters, however, may declare that the universe itself is a great living, threatening koan challenging your solution, and that when the key to this great koan is successfully discovered all other koans are minor ones and solve themselves, and, therefore, that the main thing in the study of Zen is to know the universe itself and not the problem of koan as set forward by the old masters. On the other hand, we can say this, that the universal koan is compressed in a nutshell into every one of the 'seventeen hundred koans', and when it is understood in a most thoroughgoing way the greatest one will also yield up its secrets.

In the little index finger of T'ien-lung[2] lies revealed the

---

[1] *Kung-an* in Chinese is pronounced in Japan *kō-an*; literally, it means 'a public document'. It is said that there are 1700 koans to be solved by the Zen student before he can be called a fully qualified master.

[2] *Essays in Zen Buddhism* (First Series), pp. 35–6 *f.*

mystery of the whole universe, and in the '*Kwatz*' cry of Lin-chi we hear the heavenly harmony of the spheres. However this is, I shall try in the following pages to inquire into the historical significance of the koan in Zen, its office in the realization of satori, its psychological aspect, its relation to the Nembutsu[1] as a form of the Buddhist experience, etc.

That the ultimate aim of Zen discipline is to attain what is known as 'Satori' in Japanese, and 'Sambodhi' or 'abhisamaya' (enlightenment) in Sanskrit, has already been explained in my previous writings. The *Lankāvatāra Sūtra* as a Zen text naturally emphasizes the importance of Satori, which is defined here as the *svapratyātmāryajñānagatigocara*, that is to say, 'the state of consciousness in which Noble Wisdom realizes its own inner nature'. And this self-realization constitutes the truth of Zen, which is emancipation (*moksha*) and freedom (*vaśavartin*). In order to make clear what is meant by self-realization, let me quote from the *Avataṁsaka Sūtra*:[2]

'Sudhana asked: How does one come to this emancipation face to face? How does one get this realization?

'Sucandra answered: A man comes to this emancipation face to face when his mind is awakened to Prajñāpāramitā[3] and stands in a most intimate relationship to it; for then he attains self-realization in all that he perceives and understands.

'Sudhana: Does one attain self-realization by listening to the talks and discourses on Prajñāpāramitā?

'Sucandra: That is not so. Why? Because Prajñāpāramitā sees intimately into the truth and reality of all things.

---

[1] *Buddhānusmṛiti* in Sanskrit and *nien-fo* in Chinese. It has a technical sense in Japanese Buddhism, and its relation to the koan exercise is discussed in the second part of this article.

[2] The forty-fascicle *Avataṁsaka*: Fas. XXXII. The passages quoted here do not occur in any other *Avataṁsakas*, nor in the Sanskrit *Gaṇḍavyūha*. The forty-fascicle one being a later compilation contains much additional material.

[3] Prajñāpāramitā and Aryajñāna may be considered synonyms.

'Sudhana: Is it not that thinking comes from hearing and that by thinking and reasoning one comes to perceive what Suchness is? And is this not self-realization?

'Sucandra: That is not so. Self-realization never comes from mere listening and thinking. O son of a good family, I will illustrate the matter by analogy. Listen! In a great desert there are no springs or wells; in the spring-time or in the summer when it is warm, a traveller comes from the west going eastward; he meets a man coming from the east and asks him: I am terribly thirsty; pray tell me where I can find a spring and a cool refreshing shade where I may drink, bathe, rest, and get thoroughly revived?

'The man from the east gives the traveller, as desired, all the information in detail, saying: When you go further east the road divides itself into two, right and left. You take the right one, and going steadily further on you will surely come to a fine spring and a refreshing shade. Now, son of a good family, do you think that the thirsty traveller from the west, listening to the talk about the spring and the shady trees, and thinking of going to that place as quickly as possible, can be relieved of thirst and heat and get refreshed?

'Sudhana: No, he cannot; because he is relieved of thirst and heat and gets refreshed only when, as directed by the other, he actually reaches the fountain and drinks of it and bathes in it.

'Sucandra: Son of a good family, even so with the Bodhisattva. By merely listening to it, thinking of it, and intellectually understanding it, you will never come to the realization of any truth. Son of a good family, the desert means birth and death; the man from the west means all sentient beings; the heat means all forms of confusion; thirst is greed and lust; the man from the east who knows the way is the Buddha or the Bodhisattva who, abiding in all-knowledge has penetrated into the true nature of all things and the reality of sameness; to quench the thirst and to be relieved of the heat by drinking of the refreshing fountain means the realization of the truth by oneself.

'Again, son of a good family, I will give you another
illustration. Suppose the Tathāgata had stayed among us
for another kalpa and used all kinds of contrivance, and,
by means of fine rhetoric and apt expressions, had succeeded
in convincing people of this world as to the exquisite taste,
delicious odour, soft touch, and other virtues of the
heavenly nectar; do you think that all the earthly beings
who listened to the Buddha's talk and thought of the nectar,
could taste its flavour?

'Sudhana: No, indeed; not they.

'Sucandra: Because mere listening and thinking will
never make us realize the true nature of Prajñāpāramitā.

'Sudhana: By what apt expressions and skilful illus-
trations, then, can the Bodhisattva lead all beings to the
true understanding of Reality?

'Sucandra: The true nature of Prajñāpāramitā as
realized by the Bodhisattva—this is the true definitive
principle from which all his expressions issue. When this
emancipation is realized he can aptly give expression to it
and skilfully illustrate it.'

From this we can distinctively conceive that Prajñāpāramitā which emancipates is something which must be
personally experienced by us, and that mere hearing about
it, mere learning of it, does not help us to penetrate into the
inner nature of Reality itself. Why, one may ask, cannot
the truth of self-realization be made graspable by means of
knowledge? This is answered in another place in the
Avataṁsaka Sūtra[1] by Śilpābhijñā to the following effect:

'The truth of self-realization [and Reality itself] are
neither one nor two. Because of the power of this self-
realization, [Reality] is able universally to benefit others
as well as oneself; it is absolutely impartial, with no idea
of this and that, like the earth from which all things grow.
Reality itself has neither form nor no-form; like space it is
beyond knowledge and understanding; it is too subtle to
be expressed in words and letters.

'Why? Because it is beyond the realm of letters, words,

[1] The forty-fascicle one, Fas. XXXI. This is also a later addition.

speeches, mere talk, discriminative intellection, inquiring and speculative reflection; and again it is beyond the realm of the understanding which belongs to the ignorant, beyond all evil doings which are in accordance with evil desires. Because it is neither this nor that, it is beyond all mentation; it is formless, without form, transcending the realm of all falsehoods; because it abides in the quietness of no-abode which is the realm of all holy ones.

'O son of a good family, the realm of self-realization where all the wise ones are living is free from materiality, free from purities as well as from defilements, free from grasped and grasping, free from murky confusion; it is most excellently pure and in its nature indestructible; whether the Buddha appears on earth or not, it retains its eternal oneness in the Dharmadhātu. O son of a good family, the Bodhisattva because of this truth has disciplined himself in innumerable forms of austerities, and realizing this Reality within himself has been able to benefit all beings so that they find herein the ultimate abode of safety. O son of a good family, truth of self-realization is validity itself, something unique, reality-limit, the substance of all-knowledge, the inconceivable, non-dualistic Dharmadhātu, and the perfection of emancipation in which all the arts find their complete expression.'

Further down in the forty-fascicle *Avataṁsaka*[1] we read this:

'Sudhana: Where is the abode of all Bodhisattvas?

'Mañjuśrī: In the most excellent ultimate truth they have their abode. This is the truth that knows neither birth nor death, neither loss nor destruction, neither going nor coming; these are all words, and the truth has nothing to do with words; it is far beyond them, it is impossible to be described, it has nothing to do with idle reasoning and philosophical speculation. As it has from the first no words to express itself, it is essentially quiet, realizable only in the inner consciousness of the wise.' . . .

---

[1] Fas. XXXVIII. This is again missing in the other *Avataṁsakas* and in the *Gaṇḍavyūha*.

The distinction between mere learning or mere philoso-
phizing and self-realization, between what is taught and
teachable in words and what altogether transcends one's
verbal expressions as it is to be innerly experienced—this
distinction which is fundamental has been strongly insisted upon by the Buddha; and all his followers have never
forgotten to emphasize this distinction so that the state of
self-realization which they desired would never be lost
sight of. They have, therefore, been taught to be always
intensely vigilant over themselves as if their heads were on
fire, or as if a poisonous arrow had deeply penetrated into
their flesh. They have been urged strongly to endure what is
unendurable, to practise what is the most difficult to practise in the life of an ascetic, in order that they may thus
finally come to the realization of the highest truth which
liberates them from the bondage of existence.

The importance of self-realization in the Buddhist life
has thus been recognized by all the faithful followers of the
Buddha, regardless of their doctrinal differentiations,
Hīnayāna and Mahāyāna. However inexplicable and inexpressible the truth of self-realization is, all the teachings
of Buddhism have centred around it, and Zen, as inheriting
all that is innerly realizable in Buddhism, has faithfully
transmitted its tradition by upholding satori against
ritualism and erudition and all forms of mere philoso-
phizing. If not for this fact, what is the use of the Buddha's
appearing on earth? What is the meaning of all the discipline, of all the moral and spiritual exercises?

The following sermon by Szŭ-hsin Wu-hsin of Huang-
lung (1044–1115)[1] gives vent to what is going on in the
heart of every genuine student of Zen:

'O Brethren, to be born as a human being is a rare event,
and so is the opportunity to listen to discourses on Buddhism. If you fail to achieve emancipation in this life, when
do you again expect to achieve it? While still alive, be
therefore assiduous in practising Dhyāna. The practice

[1] Quoted from the *Zen-kwan Saku-shin* (*ch'an-kuan t'sê-chin*). More about
this interesting book later on.

consists in abandonments. "The abandonment of what?" you may ask. Abandon your four elements (*bhūta*), abandon your five aggregates (*skandha*), abandon all the workings of your relative consciousness (*karmavijñāna*), which you have been cherishing since eternity; retire within your inner being and see into the reason of it. As your self-reflection grows deeper and deeper, the moment will surely come upon you when the spiritual flower will suddenly burst into bloom, illuminating the entire universe. The experience is incommunicable, though you yourselves know perfectly well what it is.

'This is the moment when you can transform this great earth into solid gold, and the great rivers into an ocean of milk. What a satisfaction this is then to your daily life! Being so, do not waste your time with words and phrases, or by searching for the truth of Zen in books; for the truth is not to be found there. Even if you memorize the whole Tripitaka as well as all the ancient classics, they are mere idle words which are of no use whatever to you at the moment of your death.'

2. The Significance of Satori in Zen

Satori is thus the whole of Zen. Zen starts with it and ends with it. When there is no satori, there is no Zen. 'Satori is the measure of Zen', as is announced by a master. Satori is not a state of mere quietude, it is not tranquillization, it is an inner experience which has a noetic quality; there must be a certain awakening from the relative field of consciousness, a certain turning-away from the ordinary form of experience which characterizes our everyday life. The technical Mahāyāna term for it is *parāvṛitti*,[1] 'turning-back' or 'turning-over' at the basis of consciousness. By this the entirety of one's mental construction goes through a complete change. It is wonderful that a satori insight is capable of causing such a reconstruction in one's spiritual

[1] *Studies in the Laṅkāvatāra Sūtra, p.* 184 *et passim.*

outlook. But the annals of Zen testify to this. The awakening
of Prajñāpāramitā, which is another name for satori, therefore, is the *sine qua non* of Zen.

There are some masters, however, who say that satori
is something artificially set up; Zen has really nothing to
do with such an excrescent growth as would injure its
natural wholesomeness; just to sit quietly—that is enough,
the Buddha is here in this doing-nothing-ness; those who
make so much fuss about satori are not real followers of
Bodhidharma. Such anti-satori masters would further
declare that the ultimate truth of Zen consists in holding on
to the Unconscious; that if anything marked with conscious
strivings comes in, this surely mars the fuller expression
of the Unconscious itself; and therefore that the ultimate
truth must not be interfered or trifled with; this is the
position taken up by some Zen advocates against the upholders of satori. As they oppose satori, they are inevitably
also against the koan exercise.

Early in the twelfth century this anti-satori and anti-
koan movement in China grew quite strong among Zen
followers of the time, and the following is a letter written
by Tai-hui[1] to his disciple Lü Chi-i,[2] warning him against
those who deny the noetic experience of satori or self-
realization:

'Lately there is an evil tendency growing up among
certain followers of Zen who regard disease as cure. As
they never had a satori in their lives, they consider it as a
sort of superstructure, a means of enticement, as something
altogether secondary in Zen, which belongs to its periphery
and not to its centre. As such teachers have never experienced a satori, they refuse to believe in those who have
actually gone through the experience. What they aim at is
to realize mere emptiness where there is no life, no noetic

---

[1] Daiye in Japanese, 1089–1163. He was one of the most outstanding
characters Zen Buddhism ever produced in the Chinese soil. He most
strongly opposed the teaching and practice of quietism, and was never
tired of upholding the importance of satori-awakening in the study of
Zen, which he felt to be nothing if not for satori.

[2] The Kōkyō Shoin Edition, T'êng, *VIII, f.* 89a.

quality whatever—that is, a blank nothingness which is regarded by them as something which is eternally beyond the limitations of time.

'In order to reach this state of utter blankness and unfathomability, they consume so many bowls of rice each day and spend their time sitting quietly and stolidly. They think this is what is meant by the attainment of absolute peace. . . . What a pity that they are altogether ignorant of the occasion when there is a sudden outburst [of intuitive knowledge in our minds]!'

The authoritative facts upon which the Zen quietists based their belief are mentioned to be as follows:[1]

'When Śākyamuni was in Magadha he shut himself up in a room and remained silent for three weeks. Is this not an example given by the Buddha in the practice of silence? When thirty-two Bodhisattvas at Vaiśālī discoursed with Vimalakīrti on the teaching of non-duality, the latter finally kept silence and did not utter a word, which elicited an unqualified admiration from Mañjuśrī. Is this not an example given by a great Bodhisattva of the practice of silence? When Subhūti sat in the rock-cave he said not a word, nor was any talk given out by him on Prajñāpāramitā. Is this not an example of silence shown by a great Śrāvaka? Seeing Subhūti thus quietly sitting in the cave, Śakrendra showered heavenly flowers over him and uttered not a word. Is this not an example of silence given by an ordinary mortal? When Bodhidharma came over to this country he sat for nine years at Shao-lin forgetful of all wordy preachings. Is this not an example of silence shown by a patriarch? Whenever Lu-tsu saw a monk coming he turned towards the wall and sat quietly. Is this not an example of silence shown by a Zen master?

'In the face of all these historic examples, how can one pronounce the practice of silent sitting as illegitimate and irrelevant in the study of Zen?'

This is the argument set forward by the advocates of Zen quietism at the time of Tai-hui in China, that is, in

[1] Daiye's discourse delivered at the request of Chien Chi-i.

the twelfth century. But Tai-hui declares that mere quiet sitting avails nothing, for it leads nowhere, as no turning-up takes place in one's mind, whereby one comes out into a world of particulars with an outlook different from the one hitherto entertained. Those quietists whose mental horizon does not rise above the level of the so-called absolute silence of unfathomability, grope in the cave of eternal darkness. They fail to open the eye of wisdom. This is where they need the guiding hand of a genuine Zen master.

Tai-hui then proceeds to give cases of satori realized under a wise instructor, pointing out how necessary it is to interview an enlightened one and to turn over once for all the whole silence-mechanism, which is inimical to the growth of the Zen mind. This up-turning of the whole system is here called by Tai-hui after the terminology of a sūtra: 'Entering into the stream and losing one's abode,' where the dualism of motion and rest forever ceases to obtain. He gives four examples:

1. When Shui-lao was trimming the wistaria, he asked his master, Ma-tsu, 'What is the idea of the Patriarch's coming over here from the West?' Ma-tsu replied, 'Come up nearer and I will tell you.' As soon as Shui-lao approached, the master gave him a kick, knocking him right down. This fall, however, all at once opened his mind to a state of satori, for he rose up with a hearty laugh, as if an event, most unexpected and most desired for, had taken place. Asked the master, 'What is the meaning of all this?' Lao exclaimed, 'Innumerable, indeed, are the truths taught by the Buddhas, all of which, even down to their very sources, I now perceive at the tip of one single hair.'

Tai-hui then comments: Lao, who had thus come to self-realization, is no more attached to the silence of Samādhi, and as he is no more attached to it he is at once above assertion and negation, and above the dualism of rest and motion. He no more relies on things outside himself but carrying out the treasure from inside his own mind exclaims, 'I have seen into the source of all truth.' The master recognizes it and does not make further remarks. When Shui-lao was later asked about his Zen understanding, he simply announced, 'Since the kick so heartily given by the master, I have not been able to stop laughing.'

2. Yun-mên asked Tung-shan: 'Whence do you come?' 'From Chia-tu.' 'Where did you pass the summer session?' 'At Pao-tzu, in Hu-nan.' 'When did you come here?' 'August the twenty-fifth.' Yun-mên concluded, 'I release you from thirty blows [though you rightly deserve them].'

On Tung-shan's interview with Mên, Tai-hui comments:

How simple-hearted Tung-shan was! He answered the master straightforwardly, and so it was natural for him to reflect, 'What fault did I commit for which I was to be given thirty blows when I replied as truthfully as I could?' The day following he appeared again before the master and asked, 'Yesterday you were pleased to release me from thirty blows, but I fail to realize my own fault.' Said Yun-mên, 'O you rice-bag, this is the way you wander from the west of the River to the south of the Lake!' This remark all of a sudden opened Tung-shan's eye, and yet he had nothing to communicate, nothing to reason about. He simply bowed, and said: 'After this I shall build my little hut where there is no human habitation; not a grain of rice will be kept in my pantry, not a stalk of vegetable will be growing on my farm; and yet I will abundantly treat all the visitors to my hermitage from all parts of the world; and I will even draw off all the nails and screws [that are holding them to a stake]; I will make them part with their greasy hats and ill-smelling clothes, so that they are thoroughly cleansed of dirt and become worthy monks.' Yun-mên smiled and said, 'What a large mouth you have for a body no larger than a coconut!'

3. Yen, the national teacher of Ku-shan, when he was still a student monk, studied for many years under Hsüeh-fêng. One day, seeing that his student was ready for a mental revolution, the master took hold of him and demanded roughly, 'What is this?' Yen was roused as if from

a deep slumber and at once comprehended what it all meant. He simply lifted his arms and swung them to and fro. Fêng said, 'What does that mean?' 'No meaning whatever, sir,' came quickly from the disciple.

4. One day Kuan-ch'i saw Lin-chi. The latter came down from his straw chair, and without saying a word seized the monk, whereupon Kuan-ch'i said, 'I know, I know.'

After enumerating these four cases Tai-hui concludes that there is after all something in Zen which can neither be imparted to others nor learned from others, and that the trouble with most people is that they are thoroughly dead and do not want to be resuscitated. Tai-hui now talks of his own experience in the following way:

I had been studying Zen for seventeen years, and during that period here and there I had fragmentary satori. I understood a little in the school of Yun-mên, and also a little in the school of Ts'ao-tung, the only trouble being that I had nowhere that decided satori in which I would find myself absolutely cut off from all time and space relations. Later I came to the capital, and staying at the T'ien-ning monastery I listened one day to my teacher's discourse on Yun-mên. He said: 'A monk came to Yun-mên and asked, "Where do all the Buddhas come from?" Yun-mên answered, "The Eastern Mountain walks on water." But I, T'ien-ning, differ from Yun-mên. "Where do all the Buddhas come from?" "A breeze laden with fragrance comes from the south, and the spacious hall begins to be refreshingly cool!"' When my master said this, I felt suddenly as if I were severed from all time and space relations. It was like cutting a skein of tangled thread with one stroke of a sharp knife. I was at the time in a perspiration all over the body.

While I ceased to feel any disturbance in my mind, I found myself to be remaining in a state of sheer serenity. When one day I saw the master in his room, he told me this: 'It is not at all easy for anybody to reach your state of mind; the only regrettable thing is that there is enough death in it but no life whatever. Not to doubt words—this is the great trouble with you. You know this well:

> ' "When thy hands are off the precipice,
>   Conviction comes upon thee all by itself;
>   Let resurrection follow death,
>   And none can now deceive thee."

'Believe me there is really such a thing as is stated here.' The master continued: 'According to my present state of mind, I am perfectly satisfied with myself and the world. All is well with me, and there is nothing of which I have to seek further understanding.'

The master then, putting me in the general dormitory, allowed me to see him three or four times a day like the lay-students of Zen. He just let me hold this, 'To be and not to be—it is like a wistaria leaning on a tree.' Whenever I wanted to speak, he at once shut me up, saying, 'Not so.' This continued for a half year, but I kept on. One day while I together with his lay-disciples was taking supper in the Fang-chang, I found myself so absorbed in the koan that I forgot to use my chopsticks to finish the supper.

The old master said, 'This fellow has only succeeded in mastering Huang-yang wood Zen, which keeps on shrinking all the time.' I then told him by a simile in what position I was. 'My position is that of a dog which stands by a fat-boiling pot: he cannot lick it however badly he wants to, nor can he go away from it though he may wish to quit.' The master said: 'That's just the case with you. [The koan] is really a vajra cage and a seat of thorns to you.'

Another day when I saw the master, I said, 'When you were with Wu-tsu, you asked him about the same koan, and what was his reply?' The master refused to give me his reply. But I insisted: 'When you asked him about it, you were not alone, you were with an assembly. It won't hurt you to tell me about it now.'

The master said: 'I asked him at the time, "To be and

not to be—it is like a wistaria leaning on a tree. What is the meaning of it?" Wu-tsu replied, "You cannot paint it, you cannot sketch it, however much you try." I further said, "What if the tree suddenly breaks down and the wistaria dies?" Wu said, "You are following the words!" '

As soon as I heard my master say this, I understood the whole thing, and said to him, 'O master, I understand.' Hearing me say that, the master remarked, 'Probably you do not.' I asked him to try me, whereupon he gave me some more koans. And every one of them was successfully answered by me. I felt that at last I was at peace with myself, for there was nothing now that obstructed my way.

3. *Chief Characteristics of Satori*

Tai-hui (Daiye) was a great advocate of satori, and one of his favourite sayings was, 'Zen has no words: when you have satori, you have everything.' Hence his strong arguments for it, which came, as has already been shown, from his own experience. Until then, he was quite ready to write a treatise against Zen in which he planned to disclaim everything accredited to Zen by its followers. His interview with his master Yüan-wu, however, rushed all his former determination, making him come out as a most intense advocate of the Zen experience. As I go on with this study of the koan exercise, I shall have many occasions to make further references to Tai-hui. In the meantime I wish to enumerate some of the most salient features of satori, which will later help us understand the role of koan in the whole structure of Zen.

1. *Irrationality.* By this I mean that satori is not a conclusion to be reached by reasoning, and defies all intellectual determination. Those who have experienced it are always at a loss to explain it coherently or logically. When it is explained at all, either in words or gestures, its content more or less undergoes a mutilation. The uninitiated are thus unable to grasp it by what is outwardly visible, while

those who have had the experience discern what is genuine
from what is not. The satori experience is thus always
characterized by irrationality, inexplicability, and incom-
municability.

Listen to Tai-hui once more: 'This matter [i.e. Zen]
is like a great mass of fire; when you approach it your
face is sure to be scorched. It is again like a sword about
to be drawn; when it is once out of the scabbard, someone
is sure to lose his life. But if you neither fling away the
scabbard nor approach the fire, you are no better than a
piece of rock or of wood. Coming to this pass, one has to be
quite a resolute character full of spirit.'[1] There is nothing
here suggestive of cool reasoning and quiet metaphysical
or epistemological analysis, but of a certain desperate will
to break through an insurmountable barrier, of the will
impelled by some irrational or unconscious power behind
it. Therefore, the outcome also defies intellection or con-
ceptualization.

2. *Intuitive insight.* That there is noetic quality in mystic
experiences has been pointed out by James in his *Varieties
of Religious Experience,* and this applies also to the Zen
experience known as satori. Another name for satori is
'ken-sho' (*chien-hsing* in Chinese) meaning 'to see essence or
nature', which apparently proves that there is 'seeing' or
'perceiving' in satori. That this seeing is of quite a different
quality from what is ordinarily designated as knowledge
need not be specifically noticed. Hui-k'ê is reported to have
made this statement concerning his satori which was confirmed by Bodhidharma himself: '[As to my satori], it is not
a total annihilation; it is knowledge of the most adequate
kind; only it cannot be expressed in words.' In this respect
Shên-hui was more explicit, for he says that 'the one
character *chih* (knowledge) is the source of all mysteries.'[2]

[1] Tai-hui's sermon at the request of Li Hsuan-chiao.
[2] *Miao* is a difficult term to translate; it often means 'exquisiteness',
'indefinable subtlety'. In this case *miao* is the mysterious way in which
things are presented to this ultimate knowledge. Tsung-mi on *Zen
Masters and Disciples.*

Without this noetic quality satori will lose all its pungency, for it is really the reason of satori itself. It is noteworthy that the knowledge contained in satori is concerned with something universal and at the same time with the individual aspect of existence. When a finger is lifted, the lifting means, from the viewpoint of satori, far more than the act of lifting. Some may call it symbolic, but satori does not point to anything beyond itself, being final as it is. Satori is the knowledge of an individual object and also that of Reality which is, if I may say so, at the back of it.

3. *Authoritativeness*. By this I mean that the knowledge realized by satori is final, that no amount of logical argument can refute it. Being direct and personal it is sufficient unto itself. All that logic can do here is to explain it, to interpret it in connection with other kinds of knowledge with which our minds are filled. Satori is thus a form of perception, an inner perception, which takes place in the most interior part of consciousness. Hence the sense of authoritativeness, which means finality. So, it is generally said that Zen is like drinking water, for it is by one's self that one knows whether it is warm or cold. The Zen perception being the last term of experience, it cannot be denied by outsiders who have no such experience.

4. *Affirmation*. What is authoritative and final can never be negative. For negation has no value for our life, it leads us nowhere; it is not a power that urges, nor does it give one a place to rest. Though the satori experience is sometimes expressed in negative terms, it is essentially an affirmative attitude towards all things that exist; it accepts them as they come along regardless of their moral values. Buddhists call this *kshānti*, 'patience', or more properly 'acceptance', that is, acceptance of things in their suprarelative or transcendental aspect where no dualism of whatever sort avails.

Some may say that this is pantheistic. The term, however, has a definite philosophic meaning and I would not see it used in this connection. When so interpreted the Zen experience exposes itself to endless misunderstandings and 'defilements'. Tai-hui says in his letter to Miao-tsung: 'An ancient sage says that the Tao itself does not require special disciplining, only let it not be defiled. I would say: To talk about mind or nature is defiling; to talk about the un-fathomable or the mysterious is defiling; to practise medi-tation or tranquillization is defiling; to direct one's atten-tion to it, to think about it, is defiling; to be writing about it thus on paper with a brush is especially defiling. What then shall we have to do in order to get ourselves oriented, and properly apply ourselves to it? The precious vajra sword is right here and its purpose is to cut off the head. Do not be concerned with human questions of right and wrong. All is Zen just as it is, and right here you are to apply yourself.' Zen is Suchness—a grand affirmation.

5. *Sense of the Beyond.* Terminology may differ in different religions, and in satori there is always what we may call a sense of the Beyond; the experience indeed is my own but I feel it to be rooted elsewhere. The individual shell in which my personality is so solidly encased explodes at the moment of satori. Not, necessarily, that I get unified with a being greater than myself or absorbed in it, but that my individuality, which I found rigidly held together and de-finitely kept separate from other individual existences, becomes loosened somehow from its tightening grip and melts away into something indescribable, something which is of quite a different order from what I am accustomed to. The feeling that follows is that of a complete release or a complete rest—the feeling that one has arrived finally at the destination. 'Coming home and quietly resting' is the ex-pression generally used by Zen followers. The story of the prodigal son in the *Saddharma-puṇḍarīka* in the *Vajra-samādhi*, and also in the New Testament points to the same feeling one has at the moment of a satori experience.

As far as the psychology of satori is considered, a sense of the Beyond is all we can say about it; to call this the Beyond, the Absolute, or God, or a Person is to go further than the experience itself and to plunge into a theology or metaphysics. Even the 'Beyond' is saying a little too much. When a Zen master says, 'There is not a fragment of a tile above my head, there is not an inch of earth beneath my feet,' the expression seems to be an appropriate one. I have called it elsewhere the Unconscious, though this has a psychological taint.

6. *Impersonal Tone*. Perhaps the most remarkable aspect of the Zen experience is that it has no personal note in it as is observable in Christian mystic experiences. There is no reference whatever in Buddhist satori to such personal and frequently sexual feelings and relationships as are to be gleaned from these terms: flame of love, a wonderful love shed in the heart, embrace, the beloved, bride, bridegroom, spiritual matrimony, Father, God, the Son of God, God's child, etc. We may say that all these terms are interpretations based on a definite system of thought and really have nothing to do with the experience itself. At any rate, alike in India, China, and Japan, satori has remained thoroughly impersonal, or rather highly intellectual.

Is this owing to the peculiar character of Buddhist philosophy? Does the experience itself take its colours from the philosophy or theology? Whatever this is, there is no doubt that in spite of its having some points of similitude to the Christian mystic experience, the Zen experience is singularly devoid of personal or human colourings. Chaopien, a great government officer of the Sung dynasty, was a lay-disciple of Fa-ch'uan of Chiang-shan. One day after his official duties were over, he found himself leisurely sitting in his office, when all of a sudden a clash of thunder burst on his ear, and he realized a state of satori. The poem he then composed depicts one aspect of the Zen experience:

'Devoid of thought, I sat quietly by the desk in my official room,
With my fountain-mind undisturbed, as serene as water;
A sudden clash of thunder, the mind-doors burst open,
And lo, there sitteth the old man in all his homeliness.'

This is perhaps all the personal tone one can find in the Zen experience, and what a distance between 'the old

man in his homeliness' and 'God in all his glory', not
to say anything about such feelings as 'the heavenly sweet-
ness of Christ's excellent love', etc.! How barren, how un-
romantic satori is when compared with the Christian
mystic experiences!

Not only satori itself is such a prosaic and non-glorious
event, but the occasion that inspires it also seems to be un-
romantic and altogether lacking in super-sensuality.
Satori is experienced in connection with any ordinary
occurrence in one's daily life. It does not appear to be an
extraordinary phenomenon as is recorded in Christian
books of mysticism. Someone takes hold of you, or slaps
you, or brings you a cup of tea, or makes some most commonplace remark, or recites some passage from a sūtra
or from a book of poetry, and when your mind is ripe for its
outburst, you come at once to satori. There is no romance
of love-making, no voice of the Holy Ghost, no plenitude
of Divine Grace, no glorification of any sort. Here is
nothing painted in high colours, all is grey and extremely
unobtrusive and unattractive.

7. *Feeling of Exaltation.* That this feeling inevitably
accompanies satori is due to the fact that it is the breaking-
up of the restriction imposed on one as an individual being,
and this breaking-up is not a mere negative incident but
quite a positive one fraught with signification because it
means an infinite expansion of the individual. The general
feeling, though we are not always conscious of it, which
characterizes all our functions of consciousness, is that of
restriction and dependence, because consciousness itself is
the outcome of two forces conditioning or restricting each
other. Satori, on the contrary, essentially consists in doing
away with the opposition of two terms in whatsoever sense
—and this opposition is the principle of consciousness as
before mentioned, while satori is to realize the Unconscious
which goes beyond the opposition.

To be released of this, therefore, must make one feel
above all things intensely exalted. A wandering outcast
maltreated everywhere not only by others but by himself

finds that he is the possessor of all the wealth and power that is ever attainable in this world by a mortal being—if this does not give him a high feeling of self-glorification, what could? Says a Zen master, 'When you have satori you are able to reveal a palatial mansion made of precious stones on a single blade of grass; but when you have no satori, a palatial mansion itself is concealed behind a simple blade of grass.'

Another Zen master, evidently alluding to the *Avataṁsaka*, declares: 'O monks, lo and behold! a most auspicious light is shining with the utmost brilliancy all over the great chiliocosm, simultaneously revealing all the countries, all the oceans, all the Sumerus, all the suns and moons, all the heavens, all the lands—each of which number as many as hundreds of thousands of kotis. O monks, do you not see the light?' But the Zen feeling of exaltation is rather a quiet feeling of self-contentment; it is not at all demonstrative, when the first glow of it passes away. The Unconscious does not proclaim itself so boisterously in the Zen consciousness.

8. *Momentariness.* Satori comes upon one abruptly and is a momentary experience. In fact, if it is not abrupt and momentary, it is not satori. This abruptness (*tun*) is what characterizes the Hui-nêng school of Zen ever since its proclamation late in the seventh century. His opponent Shên-hsiu was insistent on a gradual unfoldment of Zen consciousness. Hui-nêng's followers were thus distinguished as strong upholders of the doctrine of abruptness. This abrupt experience of satori, then, opens up in one moment (*ekamuhūrtena*) an altogether new vista, and the whole existence is appraised from quite a new angle of observation. Tung-shan's utterance, which was quoted elsewhere, amply testifies to this fact. Bukkō Kokushi's *Udāna*[1] too is suggestive in this respect.

---

[1] The First Series, pp. 255, 6, 7.

4. *Psychological Antecedents of Satori Prior to the Koan System—Some Practical Examples*

Before proceeding further to see how the koan exercise came to be recognized as the necessary step towards the realization of satori in Zen Buddhism, I wish to inquire into the psychological equipments of those Zen masters who flourished before the time of the koan. When I speak of this as something indispensable in the mastery of modern Zen, it may be asked why it is so and what was done by the ancient masters prior to the development of the koan. The koan came in vogue towards the end of the ninth century—that is, about one hundred and fifty years after Hui-nêng.

During these years Zen was practised, satori was realized, and the transmission of the Buddha-mind successfully went on. No koans were needed for the masters to train their disciples. How did they come to the Zen realization? A state of things quite different from what we see in these modern days must have then prevailed. What are the conditions of the difference? This kind of inquiry is needed to elucidate the nature of koan, to find out what psychological role it plays in the Zen experience, and finally to see in what relationship it stands to the Nembutsu, which is the essence of the Pure Land teaching.

Here I wish to see what are these psychological equipments or antecedents that lead up to satori. As we have already seen, this state or what may be called Zen consciousness comes on in connection with the most trivial incidents such as the raising of a finger, uttering a cry, reciting a phrase, swinging a stick, slapping a face, and so on. As the outcome is apparently incongruous with the occasion, we naturally presume some deep-seated psychological antecedents which are thereby abruptly brought to maturity. What are these antecedents? Let us examine a few of the classical cases of satori as recorded in the annals of Zen.

The study of these antecedents is important, for there is no doubt that they determine the nature of the experience, and, from the practical point of view, the Zen masters can thereby give the necessary instructions to their pupils in the understanding of Zen. Among the questions that may be asked here are the following: What are the intellectual factors, if there are any, in the ripening of Zen consciousness? Has the will anything to do with the experience? Is there anything approaching auto-suggestion?

In the following pages I shall try to construct something definite and tangible in the psychological history of satori. This is in a way not an easy task, as there are no autobiographical records of any sort before the koan exercise came into vogue, nor are there any detailed and accurate objective observations on the process of consciousness prior to the outburst of satori. But something constructive may be gathered up even from the vague and fragmentary records left by the Chinese when they are sympathetically analysed.

1. The story of the interview of Hui-k'ê with Bodhidharma, the first patriarch of Zen in China, is somewhat veiled with historical inaccuracies and suffers much from its dramatic treatment, but even with these disadvantages we still have an intelligent account of the interview. For historical accuracy is not always the necessary condition for determining what actually took place. Whatever literary treatment the event receives later on also helps to understand the situation. We may well remember that the imagination often depicts so-called facts psychologically more truthfully than the historian's objective narration.

According to *The Transmission of the Lamp* Hui-k'ê (or Hui-k'o, 487–593)[1] was a liberal-minded, open-hearted sort of person, thoroughly acquainted with Confucian and Taoist literature, but always dissatisfied with their teachings because they appeared to him not quite thoroughgoing. When he heard of Bodhidharma coming from India, he went to Shao-lin Szŭ where the master stayed. He

[1] The First Series, p. 191.

tried to get a chance to talk with him on the subject upon which he wished to be enlightened, but the master was always found sitting silently facing the wall.

Hui-k'ê reflected: 'History gives examples of ancient truth-seekers, who were willing for the sake of enlightenment to have the marrow extracted from their bones, their blood spilled to feed the hungry, to cover the muddy road with their hair, or to throw themselves into the mouth of a hungry tiger. What am I? Am I not also able to give myself up on the altar of truth?'

On the ninth of December of the same year, he stood in the fast-falling snow and did not move until the morning when the snow had reached his knees. Bodhidharma then took pity on him and said, 'You have been standing in the snow for some time, and what is your wish?'

Replied Hui-k'ê, 'I am come to receive your invaluable instruction; pray open the gate of mercy and extend your hand of salvation to this poor suffering mortal.'

Bodhidharma then said: 'The incomparable teaching of the Buddha can be comprehended only after a long and hard discipline and by enduring what is most difficult to endure and by practising what is most difficult to practise. Men of inferior virtue and wisdom who are light-hearted and full of self-conceit are not able even to set their eyes on the truth of Buddhism. All the labour of such men is sure to come to naught.'

Hui-k'ê was deeply moved, and in order to show his sincerity in the desire to be instructed in the teachings of all the Buddhas, he cut off his left arm with the sword he carried and presented it before the quietly meditating Bodhidharma. Thereupon, the master remarked, 'You are not to seek this [truth] through others.'

'My soul is not yet pacified. Pray, Master, pacify it.'

'Bring your soul here and I will have it pacified,' said Bodhidharma.

After a short hesitation, Hui-k'e finally confessed, 'I have sought it for many years and am still unable to take hold of it.'

Here Tai-hui makes the comment: 'Hui-k'ê well understood the situation in which he found himself after studying all the scriptures, and it was good of him that he gave the master a straightforward answer. The "thing", he knew, was not to be sought after with a purpose, or without a purpose; nor was it to be reached by means of words, nor by mere quietude; nor was it to be logically grasped, nor illogically explained. It was nowhere to be encountered nor was it to be inferred from anything; no, not in the five Skandhas, not in the eighteen Dhatus. He did well in answering this way.'

'There! Your soul is pacified once for all,' Bodhidharma confirmed.

This confirmation on the part of the master at once opened Hui-k'ê's eye of satori. Tai-hui again remarks: 'It was like the dragon getting into water, or the tiger leaning against the rock. At that moment, Hui-k'ê saw not the master before him, nor the snow, nor the mind that was reaching out for something, nor the satori itself which took possession of his mind. All vanished away from his consciousness, all was emptiness. So it was said that "Loneliness reigns here, not a figure in the monastery of Shao-lin." But did Hui-k'ê remain in this emptiness? No, he was awakened abruptly to a new life. He threw himself down over the precipice, and lo, he came out fully alive from certain death. And surely he felt then the cold shivering snow piled up in the temple court. As before, his nose rested above his upper lip.'[1]

The characteristic points I wish to notice in the case of Hui-k'ê are: that he was a learned scholar; that he was not satisfied with mere scholarship but wished to grasp something innerly; that he was most earnest in his search for an inmost truth which would give peace and rest to his soul; that he was prepared to sacrifice anything for the purpose; that he devoted some years to the hard task of locating his soul so-called, for evidently he thought in accordance with the traditional view that there was a 'soul' at the centre of

[1] Tai-hui's sermon at the request of Yang-yüan.

his being and that when it was grasped he would attain the desired end; that while Hui-k'ê's interview with Bodhidharma is narrated as if it were an event of one day or one evening, it is possible that some days or months of intense mental lucubration took place between it and the master's exhortation; that the statement 'I have not been able to take hold of my soul', was not a plain statement of fact but meant that the whole being of Hui-k'ê was thrown down, that is, he reached here the end of his life as an individual existence conscious all the time of its own individuality; that he was dead unto himself when the master's remark unexpectedly revived him—this can be seen from the remark as above cited, 'Loneliness reigns here, there is not a soul in the monastery of Shao-lin.'

This 'loneliness' is an absolute loneliness in which there is no dualistic contrast of being and non-being. The cry—for it was a cry and not a proposition—that 'there is no soul to be taken hold of', could not be uttered until this state of absolute loneliness was reached. It was also just because of this realization that Hui-k'ê was able to rise from it upon Bodhidharma's remarking, 'Pacified then is your soul!' When we carefully and sympathetically follow the course of events that led up to Hui-k'ê's satori, we naturally have to fill up in the way here proposed the gaps in the record of his life. My point of view will become clearer as we proceed.

2. The case of Hui-nêng (638–713),[1] who is regarded now as the sixth patriarch of Zen in China, presents some contrasts to that of Hui-k'ê so long as Hui-nêng is made out to be an unlearned pedlar. This treatment given to Hui-nêng is in a way interesting as it reveals a certain tendency among followers of Zen who ignore learning and the study of sūtras. In Hui-nêng's case, however, there was a historical background which made him stand against his rival, Shên-hsiu,[2] who was noted for his wide knowledge and

[1] The First Series, p. 205.
[2] Died 706.

scholarship. In reality, Hui-nêng was not such an ignoramus as his followers wanted him to appear, for his sermons known as the Platform Sūtra contain many allusions to Buddhist literature. All we can say of him as regards his learning is that he was not so erudite as Shên-hsiu. According to history, his first knowledge of Zen came from the *Vajracchedikā Sūtra.* While he was peddling wood and kindling he overheard one of his patrons reading that sūtra. This inspired him and he decided to study Zen teachings under Hung-jên, the fifth patriarch of Zen. When he saw the master, the latter asked:

'Where do you come from? What do you want here?'

'I am a farmer from Hsin-chou and wish to become a Buddha.'

'So you come from the South,' said the master, 'but the southerners have no Buddha-nature in them; how could you expect to be a Buddha?'

Hui-nêng protested, 'There are southerners and there are northerners, but as to Buddha-nature, no distinction is to be made between them.'

If Hui-nêng had had no preliminary knowledge or experience of Buddhism he could not have answered like that. He worked under Hung-jên in the granary of the monastery as a rice-cleaner and not as a regular monk, and remained there for eight months. One day the fifth patriarch, wishing to decide on his successor, wished to see how much of his teaching was understood by his followers, who numbered above five hundred. The poem composed by Shên-hsiu, the most scholarly of his five hundred disciples, ran as follows:

'This body is the Bodhi-tree,
The soul is like a mirror bright;
Take heed to keep it always clean,
And let not dust collect upon it.'

Hui-nêng was not satisfied with it and composed another which was inscribed beside the learned Shên-hsiu's:

'The Bodhi is not like the tree,
The mirror bright is nowhere shining;
As there is nothing from the beginning,
Where can the dust collect itself?'[1]

So far as we can judge by these poems alone, Hui-nêng's is in full accord with the doctrine of Emptiness as taught in the *Prajñāpāramitā Sūtra*, while Shên-hsiu's, we may say, has not yet quite fully grasped the spirit of Mahāyāna Buddhism. Hui-nêng's mind, thus, from the first developed along the line of thought indicated in the *Vajracchedikā* which he learned even before he came to Hung-jên. But it is evident that he could not have composed the poem without having experienced the truth of Emptiness in himself. The first inspiration he got from the *Vajracchedikā* made him realize the presence of a truth beyond this phenomenal world. He came to Hung-jên, but it required a great deal of trained intuitive power to get into the spirit of the *Prajñāpāramitā*, and even with the genius of Hui-nêng this could not have been accomplished very easily. He must have worked very hard while cleaning rice to have delved so successfully into the secrets of his own mind.

The eight months of menial work were by no means all menial;[2] a great spiritual upheaval was going on in the

---

[1] According to the Tun-huang MS. copy of the *Platform Sūtra*, the third line reads: 'The Buddha-nature is ever pure and undefiled.' This book, compiled by Hui-nêng's disciples, has suffered a somewhat vicissitudinous fate, and the current edition differs very much from such ancient copies as the Tun-huang MS. and the Japanese edition recently recovered at the Kōshōji monastery, Kyoto.

[2] Is it not illuminating to note that Hui-nêng passed his life in a most prosaic and apparently non-religious employment while in the monastery, working up his mind to develop into the state of satori? He did not repeat the name of the Buddha, he did not worship the Buddha according to the prescribed rules of the monastery life, he did not confess his sins and ask for pardon through the grace of God, he did not throw himself down before a Buddha and offer most ardent prayers to be relieved of the eternal bond of transmigration. He simply pounded his rice so that it could be ready for his Brotherhood's consumption. This ultra commonplaceness of Hui-nêng's role in the monastery life is the beginning of the Zen discipline which distinguishes itself remarkably from that of other Buddhist communities.

mind of Hui-nêng. The reading of Shên-hsiu's poem gave him the occasion for giving utterance to his inner vision. Whatever learning, insight, and instruction he had had before were brought finally into maturity and culminated in the poem which was the living expression of his experience. His *Vajracchedikā* thus came to life in his own being. Without actually experiencing the *Prajñāpāramitā*, Hui-nêng could not have made the statement which he did to Ming, one of his pursuers after he left Hung-jên. When Ming wanted to be enlightened, Hui-nêng said, 'Think not of good, think not of evil, but see what at the moment thy own original features are, which thou hadst even before coming into existence.'

The points which I wish to note in the case of Hui-nêng are:

a. He was not a very learned man though he was in fact well acquainted with several Mahāyāna sūtras. He was decidedly not one of those scholars who could write recondite and well-informed commentaries on the sūtras and śastras. His main idea was to get into the true meaning of a text.

b. The test which first attracted his attention was the *Vajracchedikā*, which was very likely most popular in his day. This sūtra belongs to the *Prajñāpāramitā* group. It is not a philosophical work but contains deep religious truths as they represented themselves to the Indian Mahāyānist genius. They are expressed in such a way as to be almost incomprehensible to ordinary minds, as they often seem contradictory to one another, as far as their logical thoroughness is concerned. Writers of the *Prajñāpāramitā Sūtras* are never tired of warning their readers not to get alarmed with their teachings, which are so full of audacious statements.

c. The object of Hui-nêng's coming to Huang-mei-shan was to study Zen and to breathe the spirit of the *Prajñāpāramitā*, and not to turn the rice mill or to chop wood. But there is no doubt that he did a great deal of thinking within himself. Hung-jên must have noticed it and given him occasional instructions privately as well as publicly, for we cannot think that all his five hundred pupils were left to themselves to understand the deep meaning of the *Vajracchedikā,* or the *Laṅkāvatāra,* or any other Zen literature. He must have given them frequent discourses on Zen, during all of which time Hui-nêng's mind was maturing.

d. It is probable that Shên-hsiu's poem was the occasion for Hui-nêng to bring out to the surface all that was revolving about in his deep consciousness. He had been seeking for ultimate truth, or to experience in himself the final signification of the *Prajñāpāramitā.* Shên-hsiu's poem, which went against its significance, produced in Hui-nêng's inner mind a contrary effect and opened up a more direct way to the *Prajñāpāramitā.*

e. With Hui-nêng, Zen begins to shoot out its own native roots, that is to say, what used to be Indian now turns to be genuinely Chinese. Zen has become acclimatized by Hui-nêng and firmly rooted in Chinese soil. His treatment of Ming and his sermons at Fa-hsing monastery prove his originality.

f. What is most original with Hui-nêng and his school, and what distinguishes them from Shên-hsiu, is the emphasis they place upon the abruptness of satori. For this reason the school is known as *Tun-chiao,* meaning 'abrupt teaching', in contradistinction to Shên-hsiu's *Chien-chiao,* which means 'gradual teaching'. The former flourished in the south and the latter in the north, and this geographical distribution caused them to be also known as 'Southern School' (*nan-tsung*) and 'Northern School' (*pe-tsung*). The north tended to value learning and practical discipline, while the south strongly upheld the intuitive functioning of Prajñā, which takes place 'abruptly', that is, immediately without resorting to logical process.

Learning is a slow tedious journey to the goal; and even when it is thought that the goal is reached it does not go beyond conceptualism. There are always two types of mind, intuitive and ratiocinative. The intuitive type, which is generally represented by religious geniuses, is impatient over the conceptualistic tendency of the scholar. Thus naturally the abrupt school of Hui-nêng was at war in its earlier days with the gradual school of Shên-hsiu and later with the quietist movement of some of the Zen masters of the Sung. As the history of Zen proves, the abrupt school represents more truthfully the principle of Zen consciousness which has achieved such a signal development in China and Japan ever since the day of Bodhidharma. It was Hui-nêng who became conscious of this peculiarly Zen principle and did not fail to emphasize it against the sūtra-studying and the quiet-sitting type of Zen followers. In fact, the opposition between these two tendencies has been going on throughout the history of Zen.

3. Tê-shan (780–865), who is noted for his swinging a staff, was also a student of the *Vajracchedikā* before he was converted to Zen. Different from his predecessor, Hui-nêng, he was very learned in the teaching of the sūtra and was extensively read in its commentaries, showing that his knowledge of the *Prajñāpāramitā* was more systematic than was Hui-nêng's. He heard of this Zen teaching in the south, according to which a man could be a Buddha by immediately taking hold of his inmost nature. This he thought could not be the Buddha's own teaching, but the Evil One's, and he decided to go down south. In this respect his mission again differed from that of Hui-nêng. The latter wished to get into the spirit of the *Vajracchedikā* under the guidance of the fifth patriarch, while Tê-shan's idea was to destroy Zen if possible. They were both students of the *Vajracchedikā*, but the sūtra inspired them in a way diametrically opposite. Tê-shan's psychology reminds us of that of St. Paul as he walked under the summer sun along the road to Damascus.

Tê-shan's first objective was Lung-t'an where resided a Zen master called Ch'ung-hsin. On his way to the mountain he stopped at a tea-house where he asked the woman-keeper to give him some refreshments. 'Refreshment' is *tien-hsin* in Chinese, meaning, literally, 'to punctuate the mind'. Instead of setting out the requested refreshments for the tired monk-traveller, the woman asked, 'What are you carrying on your back?'

He replied, 'They are commentaries on the *Vajracchedikā.*'

'They are indeed!' said the woman. 'May I ask you a question? If you can answer it to my satisfaction, you will have your refreshments free; but if you fail, you will have to go somewhere else.'

To this Tê-shan agreed.

The woman-keeper of the tea-house then proposed the following: 'I read in the *Vajracchedikā* that the mind is obtainable neither in the past, nor in the present, nor in the future. If so, which mind do you wish to punctuate?'

This unexpected question from an apparently insignificant country-woman completely upset the knapsackful scholarship of Tê-shan, for all his knowledge of the *Vajracchedikā* together with its various commentaries gave him no inspiration whatever. The poor scholar had to go without his lunch. Not only this, he also had to abandon his bold enterprise to defeat the teachers of Zen; for when he was no match even for the keeper of a roadside tea-house, how could he expect to defeat a professional Zen master? Even before he saw Ch'ung-hsin, master of Lung-t'an, he was certainly made to think more about his self-imposed mission.

When Tê-shan saw Ch'ung-hsin, the master of Lung-t'an, he said, 'I have heard people talk so much of Lung-t'an (dragon's pool), yet as I see it, there is no dragon here, nor any pool.'

Ch'ung-hsin quietly said, 'You are indeed in the midst of Lung-t'an.'

Tê-shan finally decided to stay at Lung-t'an and to study Zen under the guidance of its master. One evening he was sitting outside the room quietly and yet earnestly in search of the truth. Ch'ung-hsin said, 'Why do you not come in?' 'It is dark,' replied Tê-shan. Whereupon Ch'ung-hsin lighted a candle and handed it to Shan. When Shan was about to take it, Hsin blew it out. This suddenly opened his

mind to the truth of Zen teaching. Shan bowed respect-
fully.

'What is the matter with you?' asked the master.

'After this,' Shan asserted, 'whatever propositions the
Zen masters may make about Zen, I shall never again
cherish a doubt about them.'

The next morning Tê-shan took out all his commentaries on the *Vajracchedikā*, once so valued and considered so
indispensable that he had to carry them about with him
wherever he went, committed them to the flames and
turned them all into ashes.[1]

The case of Tê-shan shows some characteristic points
differing much from those of the preceding case. Shan was
learned not only in the *Vajracchedikā* but in other depart-
ments of Buddhist philosophy such as the Abhidharmakośa
and the Yogācāra. But in the beginning he was decidedly
against Zen, and the object of his coming out of the Shu
district was to annihilate it. This at any rate was the motive
that directed the surface current of his consciousness; as to
what was going on underneath he was altogether unaware
of it. The psychological law of contrariness was undoubtedly
in force and was strengthened as against his superficial
motive when he encountered a most unexpected opponent
in the form of a tea-house keeper. His first talk with
Ch'ung-hsin concerning the Dragon's Pool (Lung-t'an)
completely crushed the hard crust of Shan's mentality, releasing all the forces deeply hidden in his consciousness.
When the candle was suddenly blown out, all that was
negated prior to this incident unconditionally reasserted
itself. A complete mental cataclysm took place. What had
been regarded as most precious was now not worth a
straw.

Afterwards, when Shan himself became a master, he
used to say to an inquirer, 'Whether you say "yes", you get
thirty blows; whether you say "no", you get thirty blows
just the same.' A monk asked him, 'Who is the Buddha?'
'He is an old monk of the Western country.' 'What is en-

[1] See also the First Series, pp. 239, 247.

lightenment?' Shan gave the questioner a blow, saying, 'You get out of here; do not scatter dirt around us!' Another monk wished to know something about Zen, but Shan roared, 'I have nothing to give, begone!'

What a contrast this is to all that had been astir in Shan's mind before his arrival at Lung-t'an! It does not require much imagination to see what sort of a mental revolution was going on in Shan's mind after his interview with the woman-keeper of the tea-house, and especially when he was sitting with his master, outwardly quiet but innerly so intensely active as to be oblivious of the approach of the darkness.

4. Lin-chi (died 866) was a disciple of Huang-po, and the founder of the school that bears his name (in Japanese, Rinzai). His Zen experience presents some interesting features which may be considered in a way typically orthodox in those days when the koan system of Zen discipline was not yet in vogue. He had been studying Zen for some years under Huang-po when the head-monk asked, 'How long have you been here?' 'Three years, sir.' 'Have you ever seen the master?' 'No, sir.' 'Why don't you?' 'Because I do not now what question to ask him.' The head-monk then told Lin-chi, 'You go and see the master and ask, "What is the principle of Buddhism?"'

Lin-chi saw the master as he was told and asked, 'What is the principle of Buddhism?' Even before he could finish the question, Huang-po gave him several blows. When the head-monk saw him coming back from the master, he inquired about the result of the interview. Said Lin-chi sorrowfully, 'I asked him and was beaten with many blows.' The monk told him not to be discouraged but to go again to the master. Lin-chi saw Huang-po three times but each time the same treatment was accorded to him, and poor Chi was not any the wiser.

Finally Chi thought it best to see another master and the head-monk agreed. The master directed him to go to Tai-yü. When Lin-chi came to Tai-yü, the latter asked, 'Where do you come from?'

D

'From Huang-po.'

'What instruction did he give you?'

'I asked him three times about the ultimate principle of Buddhism and each time he gave me several blows without any instruction. I wish you would tell me what fault I committed.'

Tai-yü said, 'No one could be more thoroughly kind-hearted than that dotard master, and yet you want to know where you were faulty.'

Thus reprimanded, Lin-chi's eye was opened to the meaning of Huang-po's apparently unkind treatment. He exclaimed, 'After all there is not much in Huang-po's Buddhism!'

Tai-yü at once seized Lin-chi's collar and said: 'A while ago you said you could not understand, and now you declare that there is not much in Huang-po's Buddhism. What do you mean by that?'

Lin-chi without saying a word probed Tai-yü's ribs three times with his fist. Tai-yü loosened his hold on Chi and remarked, 'Your teacher is Huang-po; I am not at all concerned with the whole business.'

Lin-chi returned to Huang-po who asked him, 'How is it that you are back so soon?'

'Because your kindness is much too grandmotherly.'

Huang-po said, 'When I see that fellow Tai-yü, I will give him twenty blows.'

'Don't wait to see him,' said Lin-chi, 'have it now!' So saying he gave the old master a hearty slap.

The old master laughed a hearty laugh.

What attracts our attention in the present case is Lin-chi's silence for three years, not knowing what to ask the master. This appears to me to be full of significance. Did he not come to Huang-po to study Zen Buddhism? If so, what had he been doing before the head-monk advised him to see the master? And why did he not know what to ask him? And finally what made him so thoroughly transformed after seeing Tai-yü? To my mind, Lin-chi's three years under Huang-po were spent in a vain attempt to grasp by thinking it out—the final truth of Zen. He knew full well that Zen was not to be understood by verbal means or by intellectual analysis, but still by thinking he strove for self-realization. He did not know what he was really seeking or where his mental efforts were to be directed. Indeed, if he had known the what and the where, it would have to be said that he was already in possession of something definite, and one who is in possession of something definite is not far from truly understanding Zen.

It was when Lin-chi was in this troubled state of mind, wandering about on his spiritual pilgrimage, that the head-monk from his own experience perceived that the time had come for him to give some timely advice to this worn-out truth-seeker. He gave Lin-chi an index whereby he might successfully reach the goal. When Chi was roughly handled by Huang-po, he was not surprised, nor was he angered; he simply failed to understand what the blows indicated and was grieved. On his way to Tai-yü he must have pondered the subject with all the mental powers at his command. Before he was told to ask the master concerning the ultimate truth of Buddhism, his troubled mind was reaching out for something to lean on; his arms, as it were, were stretched out in every direction to grasp something in the dark. When he was in this desperate situation, a pointer came to him in the form of 'thirty blows', and Tai-yü's remark about 'a kind-hearted dotard master', which finally led him to grasp the object at which all the pointers had been directed. If it had not been for the three years of intense mental application and spiritual turmoil and vain search for the truth, this crisis could never have been reached. So many conflicting ideas, lined with different shades of feelings, had been in *mêlée*, but suddenly their tangled skein was loosened and arranged itself in a new and harmonious order.

5. *Factors Determining the Zen Experience*

From the above examples chosen rather at random from the earlier history of Zen in China, I wish to observe the following main facts concerning the Zen experience: (1) There is a preliminary intellectual equipment for the maturing of Zen-consciousness; (2) There is a strong desire to transcend oneself, by which is meant that the true student of Zen must aspire to go beyond all the limitations that are imposed upon him as an individual being; (3) A master's guiding hand is generally found there to open the way for the struggling soul; and (4) A final upheaval takes place from an unknown region, which goes under the name of 'satori'.

1. That the content of the Zen experience is largely intellectual is easily recognizable, and also that it shows a decided non-theistic or pantheistic tendency, if the theological terms, though with a great deal of reservation, are at all applicable here. Bodhidharma's demand: 'Bring your own soul and I will have it pacified'; Hui-nêng's, 'Think not of good, nor of evil, and at that very moment what are your original features?'; Nan-yüeh's, 'When it is said to be a somewhat, one altogether misses the mark'; Ma-tsu's, 'I will tell you what, when you drink up in one draught all the water of the Western Lake'—all these utterances are characteristically non-sentimental, 'non-religious', and, if anything, simply highly enigmatical, and to a certain extent intellectual, though of course not in the technical sense. Compared with such Christian expressions as 'the glory of God', 'love of God', 'the Divine Bride', etc., the Zen experience must be judged as singularly devoid of human emotions. There is in it, on the contrary, something that may be termed cold scientific evidence or matter-of-factness. Thus in the Zen consciousness we can almost say that what corresponds to the Christian ardour for a personal God is lacking.

The Zen followers are not apparently concerned with

'trespasses', 'repentance', 'forgiveness', etc. Their mentality is more of a metaphysical type, but their metaphysics consists not of abstractions, logical acuteness, and hair-splitting analysis, but of practical wisdom and concrete sense-facts. And this is where Chinese Zen specifically differs from Indian Mahāyāna Dhyāna. Hui-nêng is generally considered, as was mentioned before, not to be especially scholarly, but his mind must have been metaphysical enough to have grasped the import of the *Vajracchedikā*, which is brimful of high-sounding metaphysical assertions. When he understood the *Prajñāpāramitā Sūtra*, the highly philosophical truth contained in it was turned into the practical question of 'Your original features even prior to your birth', and then into Ma-tsu's 'drinking up the whole river in one draught', etc.

That Zen masters were invariably students of philosophy in its broadest sense, Buddhist or otherwise, before their attention was directed to Zen, is suggestive. I say here 'Buddhist philosophy' but it is not philosophy in the strict sense of the term, for it is not the result of reasoning; especially such a doctrine as that of Emptiness is not at all the outcome of intellectual reflection, but simply the statement of direct perception in which the mind grasps the true nature of existence without the intermediary of logic. In this way '*sarvadharmānāṁ śūnyatā*' is declared.

Those who study Buddhism only from its 'metaphysical' side forget that this is no more than deep insight, that it is based on experience, and not the product of abstract analysis. Therefore, when a real truth-seeker studies such sūtras as the *Laṅkāvatāra* or the *Vajracchedikā*, he cannot lightly pass over those assertions which are made here so audaciously and unconditionally; in fact he is dazzled, taken aback, or becomes frightened. But still there is a certain power in them which attracts him in spite of himself. He begins to think about them, he desires to come in direct touch with the truth itself, so that he knows that he has seen the fact with his own eyes. Ordinary books of philosophy do not lead one to this intuition because they are no more than philosophy; whatever truth philosophy teaches is exhausted within itself, and fails to open up a new vista for the student. But in the study of Buddhist sūtras which contain the utterances of the deepest religious minds, one is inwardly drawn into the deeper recesses of consciousness; and finally one becomes convinced that those utterances really touch the ground of Reality.

What one thinks or reads is always qualified by the preposition 'of', or 'about', and does not give us the thing itself. Not mere talk about water, nor the mere sight of a spring, but an actual mouthful of it gives the thirsty complete satisfaction. But a first acquaintance with the sūtras is needed to see the way pointed and know where to look for the thing itself. Without this pointing we may be at a loss how and where to concentrate our efforts. Therefore say the sūtras, 'I am both the director [or leader] and the truth itself.'

We can thus see that the antecedent that leads to the Zen experience is not adoration, obedience, fear, love, faith, penitence, or anything that usually characterizes a good Christian soul; but it is a search for something that will give mental peace and harmony by overruling contradictions and joining tangled threads into one continuous line. Every Zen aspirant feels this constant and intense seeking for mental peace and wholeness. He generally manages to have an intellectual understanding of some sort concerning himself and the world, but this invariably fails to satisfy him thoroughly, and he feels an urge to go on deeper so that the solid ground of Reality is finally reached.

Tê-shan, for example, was content with a conceptual grasp of the doctrine of Emptiness while he was studying the *Prajñāpāramitā*, but when he heard of the southern teaching his peace was disturbed. His apparent motive for going down to the South was to smash the heretical Zen, but he must have felt all the time a hidden sense of uneasiness in his deeper consciousness though he was apparently determined to suppress the feeling by his reasoning. He failed in this, for the thing which he wished to suppress suddenly raised its head, perhaps to his great discomfort, when he was challenged by the woman-keeper of the tea-house. Finally, at Lung-t'an the blowing-out of a lighted candle placed him where he was to be from the very beginning. Consciously, he never had any idea as to this final outcome, for nothing could be planned out in this matter of Zen experience. After this, that is, after the attainment of Zen intuition, the swinging of a staff was thought by him to be the only necessary thing in directing his followers to the experience of Zen.

He never prayed, he never asked for the forgiveness of his sins, he never practised anything that popularly goes under the name of religious deeds;[1] for the bowing to the Buddha,[2] the offering of incense, the reading of the sūtras, and saying the Nembutsu[3]—these were practised just because they had been practised by all the Buddhas, and manifestly for no other reason. This attitude of the Zen master is evidenced by the remarks of Huang-po[4] when he was asked as to the reason of these pious acts.

2. This intense seeking[5] is the driving force of Zen consciousness. 'Ask and it shall be given you; seek and ye shall find; knock and it shall be opened unto you.' This is also the practical instruction leading up to the Zen experience. But as this asking or seeking is altogether subjective and the biographical records of Zen do not give much information in this regard, especially in the earlier periods of Zen history, its importance is to be inferred from various circumstances connected with the experience. The presence and intensity of this seeking or inquiring spirit was

[1] When Chao-chou was asked what constituted the deeds to be properly performed by a monk, he said, 'Be detached from the deeds.'

[2] A monk came to Chao-chou and said, 'I am going as a pilgrim to the South, and what advice would you be good enough to give?' Said the master, 'If you go south, pass quickly away from where the Buddha is, nor do you stay where there is no Buddha.'

[3] A monk asked Ta-kuan of Chin-shan, 'Do you ever practise the Nembutsu ("reciting the name of the Buddha")?' The master replied, 'No, I never do.' 'Why do you not?' 'For I am afraid of polluting the mouth.'

[4] For Yao-shan's remark see elsewhere.

[5] This 'seeking' is technically known as kufū in Japanese and kung-fu in Chinese.

visible in Hui-k'ê when he was said to have stood for some time in the snow; so great was his desire to learn the truth of Zen. The biographers of Hui-nêng emphasize his lack of learning, make much of his poem on 'Emptiness', and neglect to depict his inner life during the months he was engaged in cleaning rice. His long and hazardous travelling from the south to the monastery where Hung-jên resided must have been a great undertaking in those days, the more so when we know that he was only a poor farmer's boy. His reading of the *Vajracchedikā*, or his listening to it as recorded in his biography, must have stirred up a very strong desire to know really what it all meant. Otherwise, he would not have dared such a venturesome journey; and thus, while working in the granary his mind must have been in a great state of spiritual excitement, being most intensely engaged in the search for truth.

In the case of Lin-chi, he did not even know what to ask of the master. If he had known, things would have gone probably much easier with him. He knew that there was something wrong with him, for he felt dissatisfied with himself; he was searching for some unknown reality, he knew not what. If he could define it, this meant that he had already come to its solution. His mind was just one great question-mark with no special object; as his mind was, so was the universe; just the mark, and nowhere to affix it, as there was yet nothing definite anywhere.

This groping in the dark must have lasted for some time in a most desperate manner. It was indeed this very state of mind that made him ignorant as to what specific question he might place before his master. He was not in this respect like Hui-nêng who already had a definite proposition to solve, even before he came to Hung-jên; for his problem had been the understanding of the *Vajracchedikā*. Hui-nêng's mind was perhaps the simpler and broader, while Lin-chi like Hui-k'ê was already too intellectually 'tainted', as it were; and all they felt was a general uneasiness of mind, as they knew not how to cut asunder all the entanglements which were made worse by their very learning. When the

head-monk told Lin-chi to ask the master about 'the fundamental principle of Buddhism', it was a great help indeed,
for now he had something definite to take hold of. His
general mental uneasiness was brought to an acute point,
especially when he was repulsed with 'thirty blows'. The
fruit of his mental seeking was maturing and ready to fall
on the ground.

The final shaking—quite a severe one, it must be admitted—was given by Huang-po. Between this shaking
and the final fall under Tai-yü, Lin-chi's question-mark
pointed to one concrete fact where all his three years of
accumulated efforts were most intensely concentrated.
Without this concentration he could not have exclaimed,
'There is not much after all in the Buddhism of Huang-
po!'

It may not be inopportune to say a few words concerning auto-suggestion with which the Zen experience is often
confused. In auto-suggestion there is no intellectual antecedent, nor is there any intense seeking for something,
accompanied by an acute feeling of uneasiness. In auto-
suggestion a definite proposition is given to the subject,
which is accepted by him unquestioningly and whole-
heartedly. He has a certain practical result in view, which
he desires to produce in himself by accepting the proposition. Everything is here from the first determined, prescribed, and suggested.

In Zen there is an intellectual quest for ultimate truth
which the intellect fails to satisfy; the subject is urged to
dive deeper under the waves of the empirical consciousness. This diving is beset with difficulties because he does
not know how and where to dive. He is at a complete loss
as to how to get along, until suddenly he somehow hits a
spot that opens up a new field of vision. This mental *impasse*,
accompanied by a steady, untiring, and whole-hearted
'knocking', is a most necessary stage leading to the Zen
experience. Something of the psychology of auto-suggestion
may be working here as far as its mechanical process is concerned, but the entire form into which this psychology is

fitted to work is *toto caelo* different from what is ordinarily understood by that term.

The metaphysical quest which was designated as an intellectual antecedent of Zen consciousness opens up a new course in the life of a Zen student. The quest is attended by an intense feeling of uneasiness, or one can say that the feeling is intellectually interpreted as a quest. Whether the quest is emotionally the sense of unrest, or whether the unrest is intellectually a seeking for something definite—in either case the whole being of the individual is bent on finding something upon which he may peacefully rest. The searching mind is vexed to the extreme as its fruitless strivings go on, but when it is brought up to an apex it breaks or it explodes and the whole structure of consciousness assumes an entirely different aspect. This is the Zen experience. The quest, the search, the ripening, and the explosion—thus proceeds the experience.

This seeking or quest is generally done in the form of meditation which is less intellectual (*vipaśyanā*) than concentrative (*dhyāna*). The sitter sits cross-legged after the Indian fashion as directed in the tract called *Tso-ch'an I,* 'How to sit and meditate.'

In this position, which is regarded by Indians and Buddhists generally as being the best bodily position to be assumed by the Yogins, the seeker concentrates all his mental energy in the effort to get out of this mental *impasse* into which he had been led. As the intellect has proved itself unable to achieve this end, the seeker has to call upon another power if he can find one. The intellect knows how to get him into this *cul-de-sac,* but it is singularly unable to get him out of it.

At first the seeker knows of no way of escape, but get out he must by some means, be they good or bad. He has reached the end of the passage and before him there yawns a dark abyss. There is no light to show him a possible way to cross it, nor is he aware of any way of turning back. He is simply compelled to go ahead. The only thing he can do in this crisis is simply to jump, into life or death. Perhaps it means certain death, but living he feels to be no longer possible. He is desperate, and yet something is still holding him back; he cannot quite give himself up to the unknown.

When he reaches this stage of Dhyāna, all abstract reasoning ceases; for thinker and thought no longer stand contrasted. His whole being, if we may say so, is thought itself. Or perhaps it is better to say that his whole being is 'no-thought' (acitta). We can no longer describe this state of consciousness in terms of logic or psychology. Here begins a new world of personal experiences, which we may designate 'leaping', or 'throwing oneself down the precipice'. The period of incubation has come to an end.

It is to be distinctly understood that this period of incubation, which intervenes between the metaphysical quest and the Zen experience proper, is not one of passive quietness but of intense strenuousness, in which the entire consciousness is concentrated at one point. Until the entire consciousness really gains this point, it keeps up an arduous fight against all intruding ideas. It may not be conscious of the fighting, but an intense seeking, or a steady looking-down into the abysmal darkness, is no less than that. The one-pointed concentration (ekāgra) is realized when the inner mechanism is ripe for the final catastrophe. This takes place, if seen only superficially, by accident, that is, when there is a knocking at the eardrums, or when some words are uttered, or when some unexpected event takes place, that is to say, when a perception of some kind goes on.

We may say that here a perception takes place in its purest and simplest form, where it is not at all tainted by intellectual analysis or conceptual reflection. But an epistemological interpretation of Zen experience does not interest the Zen Yogin, for he is ever intent upon truly understanding the meaning of Buddhist teachings, such as the doctrine of Emptiness or the original purity of the Dharmakāya, and thereby gaining peace of mind.

3. When the intensification of Zen consciousness is going on, the master's guiding hand is found helpful to bring about the final explosion. As in the case of Lin-chi, who did

not even know what question to ask of Huang-po, a student of Zen is frequently at a loss what to do with himself. If he is allowed to go on like this, the mental distraction may end disastrously. Or his experience may fail to attain its final goal, since it is liable to stop short before it reaches the stage of the fullest maturity. As frequently happens, the Yogin remains satisfied with an intermediate stage, which from his ignorance he takes for finality. The master is needed not only for encouraging the student to continue his upward steps but to point out to him where his goal lies.

As to the pointing, it is no pointing as far as its intelligibility is considered. Huang-po gave Lin-chi 'thirty blows', Lung-t'an blew out the candle, and Hui-nêng demanded Ming's original form even before he was born. Logically, all these pointers have no sense, they are beyond rational treatment. We can say that the pointers have no earthly use as they do not give us any clue from which we can start our inference. But inasmuch as Zen has nothing to do with ratiocination, the pointing need not be a pointing in its ordinary sense. A slap on the face, a shaking one by the shoulder, or an utterance will most assuredly do the work of pointing when the Zen consciousness has attained a certain stage of maturity.

The maturing on the one hand, therefore, and the pointing on the other must be timely; if the one is not quite matured, or if the other fails to do the pointing, the desired end may never be experienced. When the chick is ready to come out of the egg-shell, the mother hen knows and pecks at it, and lo, there jumps out a second generation of the chicken family.

We can probably state in this connection that this pointing or guiding, together with the preliminary more or less philosophical equipment of the Zen Yogin, determines the content of his Zen consciousness, and that when it is brought up to a state of full maturity it inevitably breaks out as Zen experience. In this case, the experience itself, if we can have it in its purest and most original form, may be said to be something entirely devoid of colourings of any sort,

Buddhist or Christian, Taoist or Vedantist. The experience may thus be treated wholly as a psychological event which has nothing to do with philosophy, theology, or any special religious teaching. But the point is whether, if there were no philosophical antecedent or religious aspiration or spiritual unrest, the experience could take place merely as a fact of consciousness.

The psychology, then, cannot be treated independently of philosophy or a definite set of religious teachings. That the Zen experience takes place at all as such, and is formulated finally as a system of Zen intuitions, is principally due to the master's guiding, however enigmatical it may seem; for without it the experience itself is impossible.

This explains why the confirmation of the master is needed regarding the orthodoxy of the Zen experience, and also why the history of Zen places so much stress on the orthodox transmission of it. So we read in the *Platform Sūtra* of Hui-nêng:

'Hsüan-chiao (d. A.D. 713)[1] was particularly conversant with the teaching of the T'ien-tai school on tranquillization (*śamatha*) and contemplation (*vipaśyanā*). While reading the *Vimalakīrti*, he attained an insight into the ground of consciousness. Hsüan-t'sê, a disciple of the patriarch, happened to call on him. They talked absorbingly on Buddhism, and Hsüan-t'sê found that Hsüan-chiao's remarks were in complete agreement with those of the Zen Fathers, though Chiao himself was not conscious of it. T'sê asked, "Who is your teacher in the Dharma?" Chia replied: "As regards my understanding of the sūtras of the Vaipulya class I have for each its regularly authorized teacher. Later while studying the *Vimalakīrti*, by myself I gained an insight into the teaching of the Buddha-mind, but I have nobody yet to confirm my view." T'sê said, "No confirmation is needed prior to Bhīshmasvara-rāja,[2] but after him those who have

---

[1] *See* First Series, p. 223.

[2] *Wei-yin-wang*. This may be considered to mean 'prior to the dawn of consciousness' or 'the time before any systematic teaching of religion started'.

satori by themselves with no master belong to the naturalistic school of heterodoxy." Chiao asked "Pray you testify." T'sê said, however: "My words do not carry much weight. At T'sao-ch'i the Sixth Patriarch is residing now, and people crowd upon him from all quarters to receive instruction in the Dharma. Let us go over to him". . . .'[1]

4. If the intensified Zen consciousness does not break out into the state of satori, we can say that the intensification has not yet attained its highest point; for when it does there is no other way left to it than to come to the final *dénouement* known as satori. This fact, as we have already seen, has been specially noticed by Tai-hui as characterizing the Zen experience. For, according to him, there is no Zen where there is no satori. That satori came to be recognized thus as the Zen experience *par excellence* at the time of Tai-hui and even previously, and that Tai-hui and his school had to uphold it so strongly against some tendencies which grew up among Zen followers and threatened to undermine the life of Zen, prove that the development of the koan exercise was something inevitable in the history of Zen consciousness—so inevitable indeed that if this failed to develop Zen itself would have ceased to exist.

6. *The Psychological Antecedent and the Content of the Zen Experience*

Since the early days of Zen, its practice has been mistakenly regarded as that of mere quietism or a kind of technics of mental tranquillization. Hence Hui-nêng's expostulation about it and Nan-yüeh's warning to Ma-tsu.[2] The sitting cross-legged is the form of Zen, while inwardly the Zen consciousness is to be nursed to maturity. When it is fully matured, it is sure to break out as satori, which is an

---

[1] This whole passage does not occur in the Tun-huang MS. It is probable that it was added at a much later date. But this fact does not affect the force of the argument advanced by Hsüan-t'sê.

[2] First Series, p. 237 *ff.*

insight into the Unconscious. There is something noetic in the Zen experience, and this is what determines the entire course of Zen discipline. Tai-hui was fully conscious of this fact and was never tired of upholding it against the other school.

That satori or Zen experience is not the outcome of quiet-sitting or mere passivity, with which Zen discipline has been confused very much even by the followers of Zen themselves, can be inferred from the utterances or gestures that follow the final event. How shall we interpret Lin-chi's utterance, 'There is not much in the Buddhism of Huang-po'? Again, how about his punching the ribs of Tai-yü? These evidently show that there was something active and noetic in his experience. He actually grasped something that met his approval.

There is no doubt that he found what he had all the time been searching for, although at the moment when he began his searching he had no idea of what it meant—for how could he? If he remained altogether passive, he could never have made such a positive assertion. As to his gesture, how self-assuring it was, which grew out of his absolute conviction! There is nothing whatever passive about it.[1]

The situation is well described by Dai-o Kokushi when he says: 'By a "special transmission outside the sūtra-teaching" is meant to understand penetratingly just one

[1] One day St. Francis was sitting with his companions when he began to groan and said, 'There is hardly a monk on earth who perfectly obeys his superior.' His companions much astonished said, 'Explain to us, Father, what is perfect and supreme obedience.' Then, comparing him who obeys to a corpse, he said: 'Take a dead body and put it where you will, it will make no resistance: when it is in one place it will not murmur; when you take it away from there it will not object; put it in a pulpit, it will not look up but down; wrap it in purple and it will only look doubly pale.' (Paul Sabatier's *Life of St. Francis*, pp. 260–1.) While it is difficult to tell what is the real purport of this, it may appear as if St. Francis wished his monks to be literally like a corpse; but there is something humorous about the remark when he says, 'Put it in a pulpit. . . .' The Zen Buddhist would interpret it as meaning to keep one's mind in a perfect state of perspicuity which perceives a flower as red and a willow-tree as green, without putting anything of its own confused subjectivity into it. A state of passivity, indeed, and yet there is also fullness of activity in it. A form of passive activity, we may call it.

phrase by breaking both the mirror and the image, by transcending all forms of ideation, by making no distinction whatever between confusion and enlightenment, by paying no attention to the presence or the absence of a thought, by neither getting attached to nor keeping oneself away from the dualism of good and bad. The one phrase which the follower of Zen is asked to ponder (*kung-fu*) and find the final solution of is "Your own original features even before you were born of your parents."

'In answering this one ought not to cogitate on the meaning of the phrase, nor try to get away from it; do not reason about it, nor altogether abandon reasoning; respond just as you are asked and without deliberation, just as a bell rings when it is struck, just as a man answers when he is called by name. If there were no seeking, no pondering, no contriving as to how to get at the meaning of the phrase, whatever it may be, there would be no answering—hence no awakening.'

While it is difficult to determine the content of Zen experience merely by means of those utterances and gestures which involuntarily follow the experience—which is, indeed, a study in itself—I give in the appendices some of them which are culled indiscriminately from the history of Zen.[1] Judging from these utterances, we can see that all these authors have had an inner perception, which put an end to whatever doubts and mental anxieties from which they may have been suffering; and further, that the nature of this inner perception did not allow itself to be syllogistically treated, as it had no logical connection with what has preceded it.

Satori as a rule expresses itself in words which are not intelligble to the ordinary mind; sometimes the expression is merely descriptive of the experience-feeling, which naturally means nothing to those who have never had such feelings within themselves. So far as the intellect is con-

---

[1] Some have already been given in my *Essays in Zen Buddhism*, Vol. I, pp. 248 *et seq.*, where I have collected more of these utterances as they stand in the original.

cerned, there is an unsurpassable gap between the antecedent problem and its consequent solution; the two are left logically unconnected. When Lin-chi asked about the ultimate principle of Buddhism, he was given thirty blows by his master Huang-po. After he had attained satori and understood the meaning of his experience, he merely said, 'There is not much in Huang-po's Buddhism.' We are left ignorant as to what this 'not much' really is. When this 'what' was demanded by Tai-yü, Lin-chi simply poked his ribs.

These gestures and utterances do not give the outsider any clue to the content of the experience itself. They seem to be talking in signs. This logical discontinuity or discreteness is characteristic of all Zen teaching. When Ch'ing-ping[1] was asked what the Mahāyāna was, he said, 'The bucket-rope.' When asked about the Hīnayāna, he replied: 'The coin-string'; about the moral impurities (*āsrava*), 'The bamboo-basket'; about the moral purities (*anāsrava*), 'The wooden dipper'. These answers are apparently nonsensical, but from the Zen point of view they are easily digested, for the logical discontinuity is thereby bridged over. The Zen experience evidently opens a closed door revealing all the treasures behind it. It suddenly leaps over to the other side of logic and starts a dialectics of its own.

Psychologically, this is accomplished when what is known as 'abandonment', 'or 'throwing oneself over the precipice', takes place. This 'abandonment' means the moral courage of taking risks; it is plunging into the unknown which lies beyond the topography of relative knowledge. This unknown realm of logical discontinuity must be explored personally; and this is where logic turns into psychology, it is where conceptualism has to give way to life-experience.

We cannot, however, 'abandon' ourselves just because we wish to do so. It may seem an easy thing to do, but after all it is the last thing any being can do, for it is done only when we are most thoroughly convinced that there is no

---

[1] *Ch'ing-ping ling-tsun*, 845–919. As regards his interview with *T'sui-wei*, see elsewhere.

E

other way to meet the situation. We are always conscious of a tie, slender enough to be sure, but how strong when we try to cut it off! It is always holding us back when we wish to throw ourselves at the feet of an all-merciful One, or when we are urged to identify ourselves with a noble cause or anything that is grander than mere selfishness. Before being able to do this there must be a great deal of 'searching', or 'contriving', or 'pondering'.[1] It is only when this process is brought to maturity that this 'abandoning' can take place. We can say that this 'contriving' is a form of purgation.

When all the traces of egotism are purged away, when the will-to-live is effectively put down, when the intellect gives up its hold on the discrimination between subject and object, then all the contrivances cease, the purgation is achieved, and the 'abandonment' is ready to take place.[2]

All Zen masters are, therefore, quite emphatic about completing the whole process of 'contriving and searching'. For an abandonment to be thoroughgoing, it is necessary for the preliminary process to be also thoroughgoing. The masters all teach the necessity of going on with this 'searching' as if one were fighting against a deadly enemy, or 'as if a poisonous arrow were piercing a vital part of the body, or as if one were surrounded on all sides by raging flames, or as if one had lost both his parents, or as if one were disgraced owing to one's inability to pay off a debt of a thousand pieces of gold'.

Shōichi Kōkushi, the founder of Tōfukuji monastery, advises one to 'think yourself to be down an old deep well; the only thought you then have will be to get out of it, and

---

[1] The Christians would say, 'a great deal of seeking, asking, and knocking'.

[2] James gives in his *Varieties of Religious Experience* (pp. 321 ff.) the story of Antoinette Bourignon, who, finding her spiritual obstacle in the possession of a penny, threw it away and started her long spiritual journey thus absolutely free from earthly cares. 'A penny' is the symbol of the last thread of egotism which so effectively ties us up to a world of relativity. Slender though the thread is, it is sufficiently strong for all of us. The cutter is given to the student of Zen in the shape of a koan, as will be seen later on.

you will be desperately engaged in finding a way of escape; from morning to evening this one thought will occupy the entire field of your consciousness'. When one's mind is so fully occupied with one single thought, strangely or miraculously there takes place a sudden awakening within oneself. All the 'searching and contriving' ceases, and with it comes the feeling that what was wanted is here, that all is well with the world and with oneself, and that the problem is now for the first time successfully and satisfactorily solved. The Chinese have the saying, 'When you are in an *impasse*, there is an opening.' The Christians teach, 'Man's extremity is God's opportunity.'

The main thing to do when a man finds himself in this mental extremity is to exhaust all his powers of 'searching and contriving', which means to concentrate all his energy on one single point and see the farthest reach he can make in this frontal attack. Whether he is pondering a knotty problem of philosophy, or mathematics, or contriving a means of escape from oppressive conditions, or seeking a passage of liberation from an apparently hopeless situation, his empirical mind, psychologically speaking, is taxed to its limit of energy; but when the limit is transcended a new source of energy in one form or another is tapped.

Physically, an extraordinary amount of strength or endurance is exhibited to the surprise of the man himself; morally, often on a battlefield a soldier manifests great courage, performing deeds of audacity; intellectually, a philosopher, if he is a really great one, clears up a new way of looking at Reality; religiously, we have such spiritual phenomena as conversion, conformation, reformation, salvation to the Christians, and satori, enlightenment, intuition, *parāvritti*, etc., to the Buddhists.

All these various orders of phenomena are explainable, as far as psychology goes, by the same law; accumulation, saturation, and explosion. But what is peculiar to the religious experience is that it involves the whole being of the individual, that it affects the very foundation of his character. And besides, the content of this experience may be described in the terminology of either Christian faith or Buddhist philosophy, according to the nature of its antecedents, or according to the surroundings and education of the particular individual concerned. That is, he interprets the experience in conformity to his own intellectual resources, and to him this interpretation is the best and the only plausible one to be given to the facts in hand.

He cannot accept them in any other light, for to do so will be the same as rejecting them as illusive and devoid of meaning. As Buddhism has no such creeds as are cherished by Christians, who are Christians because of their intellectually conforming themselves to the theology and tradition of their forefathers, Buddhists give their religious experience an altogether different colouring. Especially to Zen followers such terms as divine grace, revelation, mystic union, etc., are foreign and sound quite unfamiliar. No matter how closely psychologically related one experience may be to the other, Buddhist or Christian, it begins to vary widely as soon as it is subsumed under categories of the Christian or the Buddhist ideology.

As stated before, the antecedents of the experience are thus designated by Zen masters altogether differently from those of the Christian mystics. Stigmata, ligature, expurgation, road of the cross, the anguish of love, etc.—all such terms have no meaning in Zen experience. The antecedents required by the latter are concentration, accumulation, self-forgetting, throwing oneself down the precipice, going over to the other side of birth-and-death, leaping, abandonment, cutting off what precedes and what follows, etc. There is here absolutely nothing that may be called religious by those who are familiar only with the other set of phraseology.

To make clearer this psychological process of 'self-forgetting' and 'cutting off both the past and the future', let me cite some of the classical examples.

The monk Ting came to Lin-chi and asked, 'What is the essence of Buddhism?' Chi came down from his straw chair, seized the monk, gave him a slap, and let him go. Ting stood still. A monk nearby said, 'O Ting, why don't you make a bow?' Ting was about to bow when he came to a realization.[1]

This is the brief statement in the language of Lin-chi of the event that happened to Ting. Brief though it is, we can gather from it all that is essential, all that we need to know concerning Ting's Zen experience. First of all, he did not come to Lin-chi casually. There is no doubt that his question was the outcome of a long pondering and an anxious search after the truth. Before the koan system was yet in vogue, Zen followers did not definitely know how to ask a question, as we saw in the case of Lin-chi.

Intellectual puzzles are everywhere, but the difficulty is to produce a question which is vital and on which depends the destiny of the questioner himself. When such a question is brought to light, the very asking is more than half the answering. Just a little movement on the part of the master may be sufficient to open up a new life in the questioner. The answer is not in the master's gesture or speech; it is in the questioner's own mind which is now awakened. When Ting asked the master about the essence of Buddhism, the question was no idle one; it came out of his inmost being, and he never expected to have it answered intellectually.

When he was seized and slapped by the master, he was probably not at all surprised, in the sense that he was taken aback and at a loss what to do; but he was surprised in this sense that he was entirely put out of the beaten track of logic where he was most likely still lingering, although he was not conscious of it himself. He was carried away from the earth where he used to stand and to which he seemed to be inevitably bound; he was carried away he knew not where, only that he was now lost to the world and to himself. This was the meaning of his 'standing still'. All his former efforts to find an answer to his question were put to naught; he was at the edge of the precipice to which he clung with all his remaining strength, but the master

[1] *Lin-chi-lu.*

relentlessly pushed him over. Even when he heard the voice
of the attending monk calling out to him, he was not fully
awakened from his stupefaction. It was only when he was
about to make the usual bows that he recovered his sense—
the sense in which logical discontinuity was bridged over
and in which the answer to his question was experienced
within himself—the sense in which he read the ultimate
meaning of all existence, having nothing further to seek.

This *dénouement*, however, could not have been attained
had it not been preceded by the regular course of concentration, accumulation, and abandonment. If Ting's
question had been an abstract and conceptual one which
had no roots in his very being, there could not have been
truth and ultimacy in his understanding of the answer.

To give another illustration which will be illuminating
when considered in connection with Ting, Yün-mên[1]
(*d.* 949) was the founder of the school bearing his name.
His first master was Mu-chou, who had urged Lin-chi to
ask Huang-po concerning the essence of Buddhism. Mên
was not satisfied with his knowledge of Buddhism which
had been gained from books, and came to Mu-chou to have
a final settlement of the intellectual balance-sheet with
him. Seeing Mên approach the gate, Mu-chou shut it in his
face. Mên could not understand what it all meant, but he
knocked and a voice came from within:

'Who are you?'

'My name is Yün-mên. I come from Chih-hsing.'

'What do you want?'

'I am unable to see into the ground of my being and most
earnestly wish to be enlightened.'

Mu-chou opened the gate, looked at Mên, and then
closed it. Not knowing what to do, Mên went away. This
was a great riddle, indeed, and some time later he came
back to Mu-chou. But he was treated in the same way as
before. When Yün-mên came for a third time to Mu-chou's
gate, his mind was firmly made up, by whatever means,
to have a talk with the master. This time as soon as the

[1] *Yün-mên lu.*

gate was opened he squeezed himself through the opening. The intruder was at once seized by the chest and the master demanded: 'Speak! Speak!' Mên was bewildered and hesitated. Chou, however, lost no time in pushing him out of the gate again, saying, 'You good-for-nothing fellow!' As the heavy gate swung shut, it caught one of Mên's legs, and he cried out: 'Oh! Oh!' But this opened his eyes to the significance of the whole proceeding.

It is easy to infer from this record that Yün-mên's Zen experience had a long and arduous preliminary course, although there is in the record no allusion to his psychological attitude towards the whole affair. His 'searching and contriving' did not of course begin with this experience; it came to an end when he called on Mu-chou. He knew no means of escape from the dilemma in which he found himself; his only hope was centred in Mu-chou. But what answer did he get from the master? To be looked at and shut out—what relation could this have to his earnest questioning about his inner self?

On his way home he must have pondered the new situation to the limit of his mental capacity. This pondering, this searching must have been intensified by his second visit to the master, and on the third visit it was fast approaching a culmination, and most naturally ended dramatically. When he was requested by Mu-chou to speak out if he had anything to say, to utter a word if there was something that required expression, his Zen consciousness became fully matured, and only a touch was needed to change it into an awakening. The needed touch came in the form of an intense physical pain. His cry, 'Oh! Oh!' was at the same time the cry of satori, an inner perception of his own being, whose depth now for the first time he has personally sounded so that he could really say, 'I know, for I am it!'

(This psychological process has been depicted here somewhat conjecturely, but it will grow more convincing later when the psychology of the koan exercise is described according to the various records left by the masters, and also according to the directions given by them to their devotees.)

7. Technique of Zen Discipline in its Early History

As can readily be conceived from the foregoing delinea-
tion of the satori psychology, it is, indeed, no easy task to
develop the Zen consciousness into this culminating stage.
In the early days of Zen Buddhism in China there were
enough original minds who looked for a first-hand experience, and who never flinched from the hazardous adventure
into the *terra incognita* of Zen mysticism.

The masters at that time had no special system for leading them to the final experience except giving them some
indications in gestures or words, both of which, being altogether unapproachable, repelled rather than attracted the
truth-seekers. The path was strewn with thistles and
brambles instead of flowers, and they had to risk so much
when they wandered out into it. It was, therefore, natural
that there were only a few out of the many disciples that
gathered about a master who attained satori. Out of the
five hundred or a thousand pupils that are said to have
come to a mountain monastery presided over by a fully-
qualified Zen master, there were less than ten whose eyes
were said to have been opened to gaze into the mysterious
values of Zen. Zen was an aristocratic form of Buddhism.
Its ideal was to have one great master-mind which towered
far above the ordinary, rather than to have many medio-
crities.

The masters thus made the path of Zen as steep and as
stormy as they could so that only the tough-hearted could
scale it to the summit. This was not intentional, of course,
on their part; they had no malicious or selfish will to keep
the treasure among themselves; they naturally wanted to
see their teaching embraced as widely as possible among
their fellow-beings; they never seemed to get tired in its
propagation, but when they wanted to be true to their insight they could not stoop to appeal to popular taste, that is,
they could not give up their vocation for mere reputation
and cheap appreciation. Ching-t'sên of Chang-sha used to

say that, 'If I were to demonstrate the truth of Zen in its absolute aspect, the front court of my monastery would see weeds growing rampant.'

On the other hand, the world is generally filled with imitators, counterfeiters, dealers in second-hand articles, this not only in the commercial world but in religious circles also. Perhaps more so in the latter, because here it is less easy to distinguish the genuine from the spurious. When other practical circumstances are added to the difficulties inherent in Zen which make for its exclusion, solitude, and gradual disappearance from the world, we can see how mortified the masters must have been over the actual situation in which they often found themselves. That is, they could not sit quiet in their mountain retreats and watch the declining of the Zen spirit. There were imitators enough who swallowed the literature and left the spirit behind.

Moreover, since Hui-nêng, the sixth patriarch, there had been a steady growth of Zen literature, and the way in which Zen expressed itself grew more delicate, subtle, and varied. Gradually the one school of Hui-nêng divided itself into several branches so that in early Sung, that is, in the eleventh century, there were five of them flourishing. The time was fast approaching when Zen masters were not content just to wait and see Zen consciousness develop of its own accord. They recognized the need of some system to accelerate the development and to effect its healthful propagation and continued prosperity. They thought it was their duty to see that their Zen experience be successively transmitted from master to disciple without interruption. But before we speak of the development of this system let us first see how Zen was taught in the early days of its history.

As we know already from the examples of Lin-chi, Yün-mên, the monk Ting, and Tê-shan, the master had no special contrivance or method by which the mind of the disciple could be matured for the experience. Each no doubt occasionally gave sermons and discourses on Zen in his Dharma Hall; he also demonstrated it in most practical ways for the sake of his disciples. Zen was not a conceptual plaything with them but a vital fact which intimately concerned life itself—even in raising a finger, in sipping a cup of tea, in exchanging greetings, and so on. And to awaken the consciousness of his disciples to the truth of Zen, it was most natural for the masters to make use of every opportunity in their daily life. The following interviews recorded of the ancient masters[1] will fully illustrate what I mean.

When Hui-nêng saw Nan-yüeh approach, he asked:
'Whence comest thou?'
'I come from Tung-shan.'
'What is it that thus cometh?'

It took Nan-yüeh six years to solve this object lesson and say, 'Even when it is said to be something, the mark is already missed!'

A monk came to Ch'i-an of Yen-kuan and asked, 'Who is Vairocana Buddha?'

Said the master, 'Kindly pass that pitcher over here.'

The monk took it to the master, who then asked the monk to put it back where he got it from. He did so and then asked the master again about the Buddha.

The master replied, 'Long gone is he!'

Wu-yeh of Fêng-chou was a stalwart, athletic monk. When he came to Ma-tsu the latter remarked:

'What a magnificent structure with no Buddha in it!'

Wu-yeh made a bow and said, 'As to the literature of the Triple Vehicle, I have a general knowledge of it, but I have not yet been able to understand the teaching of Zen according to which mind is the Buddha.'

Replied the master, 'The mind that does not understand is the Buddha; there is no other.'

Yeh asked again: 'The First Patriarch is said to have brought a secret message from India. What was it?'

Ma-tsu said, 'Monk, I am very busy just now, you may come some other time.'

[1] From the *Chuan-têng-lu*.

Yeh was about to leave the room when the master called out, 'O monk!'

Yeh turned back.

'What is it?' the master said.

This awakened Wu-yeh's mind to the full understanding of Zen, and he made his bows.

'O this stupid fellow! What is the use of your making bows?' were the master's last words.

Têng Yin-fêng[1] was standing beside Shih-t'ou who was cutting weeds. When Shih-t'ou moved a bundle of grass in front of Feng, the latter said:

'You only know how to cut this down, but not the other one.'

Shih-t'ou held up the sickle.

Fêng snatched it from him and assumed the posture of a mower.

T'ou remarked, 'You cut the other one down, but know not how to cut this one down.'

Fêng made no answer.

When Wei-shan was one day in attendance on his master, Pai-chang, the master asked him:

'Who are you?'

'Ling-yu, sir.'

'Dig into the ashes and see if there is any fire in the fireplace.'

---

[1] When Fêng was about to pass away at the Vajra Cave, of Wu-tai Shan, he said: 'I have myself seen the masters pass away lying or sitting but not standing. Do you know any masters who passed away standing?' The monks said, 'Yes, there is the record of such.' 'Do you then know one who passed away standing on his head?' 'No, never yet,' was the answer. Whereupon Fêng stood on his head and passed away. His garment remained attached to his body. When people carried his body to the crematory it kept its extraordinary position unchanged. It was an object of wonder and admiration. The master had a sister who was a nun, and she happened to be among the interested crowd. She approached the corpse of the brother and reproached him saying, 'O brother! While still alive, you have not observed the laws, and after death you still try to play a trick on people.' She then poked the brother with her hand, and the dead body went down on the ground with a thud.

Shan dug into the fire-place, and said, 'No fire, sir.'

Pai-chang rose from his seat, dug deeper into the ashes, and, finding a little piece of live charcoal, held it up, and showing it to Shan, said:

'Is this not a live one?'

This opened Shan's eye.

Tai-an studied the Vinaya texts at Huang-po Shan, which, however, failed to satisfy him, for he had as yet no approach to the ultimate meaning of Buddhist truth. He went about on his disciplinary pilgrimage and came to Pai-chang. Tai-an remarked, 'I have been seeking for the Buddha, but do not yet know how to go on with my research.'

Said the master, 'It is very much like looking for an ox when riding on one.'

'What shall a man do after knowing him?'

'It is like going home on the back of an ox.'

'May I be further enlightened as to the care I shall have to bestow on the whole matter?'

Pai-chang said, 'It is like a cowherd looking after his cattle, who using his staff keeps them from wandering into another's pasture.'

When Kao was still a novice and not yet fully ordained, he came to Yao-shan.

Yao-shan said, 'Whence comest thou?'

'From Nan-yüeh, sir.'

'Whither goest thou?'

'To Chiang-ling for ordination.'

'What is your idea in getting ordained?'

'I wish to be free from birth-and-death.'

'Do you know,' said the master, 'there is one who, even without being ordained, is free from birth-and-death?'

Shan-tao was walking one day with his master in the mountains. The master, Shih-t'ou, saw the branches of a tree obstructing the pathway and requested Shan-tao to clear them away.

Said the disciple, 'I did not bring a knife with me.'

Shih-t'ou took out his own knife and held it out with the naked blade towards his disciple.

Shan-tao said, 'Please give me the other end.'

'What do you want to do with the other end?' asked the master.

This made Shan-tao wake to the truth of Zen.

From these examples taken at random from *The Transmission of the Lamp*, which is the first history of Zen, we can see that the method of the Zen masters was thoroughly practical but had no prescribed plan. If the pupil had no question of his own, the master would try to draw him out, not abstractly but out of life itself as they were living it. There were already some stock questions in circulation among followers of Zen, with which they approached the master, and there were also some favourite questions that were regularly asked by the masters. But there was nothing systematized either on the part of the master or the pupil as to the pursuance of the study of Zen.

One of the questions most frequently asked by the novitiate was concerned with the reason for Bodhidharma's visit to China. This was quite natural as Zen had originated in China with his coming from India, and those who wished to follow his steps could not but be eager to know the great message of Bodhidharma. On the other hand, the most popular question put by the masters was as to the whence and the whither of each new arrival at the monastery. 'Whence comest thou?' was not a question prompted by mere curiosity; for if we really know the whence and the whither we are already masters of Zen.

Besides these *bona fide* Zen followers, there were many Buddhist philosophers, especially in the earlier days of Zen in the T'ang dynasty, who being partial to their own philosophies were often in controversy with Zen masters. These interviews afford us an interesting spectacle which is always at the expense of the philosophers.

.   .   .   .   .

A monk came to Hui-chung and was asked, 'What is your business?'

'I discourse on the *Vajracchedikā Sūtra.*'

'Tell me what are the first two characters of the sūtra?'

'*Ju shih*' (thus, *evam*).[1]

Demanded the master, 'What does that mean?'

There was no answer.

A Buddhist philosopher called on Ma-tsu and said, 'May I ask what teaching is held by a Zen master?'

Ma-tsu, instead of answering him, proposed a counter-question, 'What teaching do you hold?'

'I have the honour of discoursing on more than twenty sūtras and śastras.'

'You are really a lion-child, are you not?'

'I feel complimented, sir.'

Ma-tsu gave out a soft long breath. Thereupon, the philosopher remarked, 'This is really it.'

'What does that mean?'

'This is the way the lion comes out of its den.'

The master remained silent.

'This also is really it,' remarked the philosopher.

'What does that mean?'

'This is the way the lion lies in his den.'

'When there is neither going-out nor coming-in, what becomes of it?'

The philosopher gave no answer. Later, when he left the master and was about to pass out of the gate, the master called out, 'O philosopher!' He turned back. Said the master, 'What is that?' There was no answer, which elicited this from Ma-tsu, 'Oh, that stupid teacher of the sūtras!'

A teacher of the *Avataṁsaka* came to see Hui-hai and asked, 'Master, do you believe that non-sentient beings are Buddhas?'

'No,' said the master, 'I do not believe so. If non-sentient

[1] Ju shih is the opening word of all the sūtras.

beings are Buddhas, living beings are worse off than the dead; dead donkeys, dead dogs will be far better than living human beings. We read in the sūtra that the Buddha-body is no other than the Dharma-body which is born of morality (*śīla*), meditation (*dhyāna*), and knowledge (*prajñā*), born of the three sciences (*vidyā*) and the six supernatural powers (*abhijñā*), born of all deeds of merit. If non-sentient beings are Buddhas, you, Reverend Sir, had better pass away this moment and attain Buddhahood.'

Another *Avataṁsaka* teacher called Chih came to Hui-hai and asked, 'Why do you not admit that the evergreen bamboos are all the Dharmakāya and that there are no thickly-blooming yellow flowers that are not Prajñā?'

Said the master: 'The Dharmakāya [in itself] has no form, but by means of the green bamboos it assumes a form; Prajñā [in itself] is devoid of sentiency, but facing the yellow flowers it functions. That there is Prajñā and Dharmakāya is not owing to the green bamboos and yellow flowers. Therefore, it is stated in the sūtra that the true Dharmakāya of the Buddha is like emptiness of space, and that like the moon reflected in water there are forms in response to individual objects. If the yellow flower is Prajñā, Prajñā is non-sentient; if the green bamboo is the Dharmakāya, the bamboo may know how to function in various relations. O Teacher, do you understand?'

'No, Master, I am unable to follow you.'

'If a man has an insight into the nature of his own being,' said the master, 'he will understand the truth in whatever way it is presented either affirmatively or negatively. He knows how not to get attached to either side since he has grasped the principle of things as they move on. But a man of no such spiritual insight is attached to the green bamboo or to the yellow flower when reference is made to either of them. He dallies with Dharmakāya when he discourses on it, he knows not what Prajñā is, even when he talks of it. Thus there is a constant wrangling among you teachers.'

This was the way Zen teaching was practised until about the tenth century. In order to facilitate the understanding of the state of affairs that had been going on during those years, let me cite what is known as 'The Eighteen kinds of Question', compiled by Shan-chao of Fên-yang.[1] He flourished towards the end of the tenth century and was a disciple of Shêng-nien of Shou-shan.[2] The classification is unscientific but the 'Questions' are illuminating in many ways as they illustrate how Zen was studied in those days.

1. The question asking for instruction. This is what is generally asked by a novice of the master, wishing to be enlightened on such subjects as Buddha, the signification of Bodhidharma's visit to China, the essence of the Buddhist teaching, the Dharmakāya, etc.

2. The question in which the questioner asks for the master's judgment by describing his own mental condition. When a monk said to Chao-chou, 'What do you say to one who has nothing to carry about?' he was analysing his own state of mind. To this Chao-chou replied, 'Carry it along.'

3. The question whereby the questioner attempts to see where the master stands. A monk came to Tung-fêng who lived in a mountain hut and asked him, 'If a tiger should suddenly appear here, what would you do?' The hut-keeper roared like a tiger; the monk behaved as if terrified; whereupon the keeper laughed heartily.

4. The question in which the questioner shows that he still has a doubt as to his attainment and expresses his desire for confirmation. A monk asked Tao-wu of T'ien-huang, 'What shall I do when there is still a shadow of doubt?' Wu replied, 'Even oneness when held on to is wide of the mark.'

5. The question whereby the questioner is anxious to find out the master's attitude. A monk asked Chao-chou, 'All things are reducible to the One; but where is the One

[1] *Jen t'ien yen mu*, 'Eyes of Men and Gods', Fas. II.
[2] A.D. 926–993.

reducible?' Chou said, 'When I was in the district of Ch'ing I had a robe made that weighed seven *chin*.'

6. The question asked by one who is at a loss as to how to go on with his study of Zen. A monk asked Hsing-hua: 'I am unable to distinguish black from white. Pray enlighten me somehow.' The question was hardly out when the master gave him a good slashing.

7. The question asked with the intention to probe into the attainment of the master. This kind of question must have been in vogue when the Zen monasteries were everywhere established and the monks travelled from one master to another. A monk asked Fêng-hsüeh, 'How is it that one who understands not, never cherishes a doubt?' Replied the master, 'When a tortoise walks on the ground, he cannot help leaving traces in the mud.'

8. The question of ignorance. This does not seem to differ from the sixth. A monk asked Hsüan-sha, 'I am a newcomer in the monastery; please tell me how to go on with my study.' 'Do you hear the murmuring stream?' 'Yes, master.' 'If so, here is the entrance.'

9. The question proposed by one who has his own view of Zen and wishes to see how the master takes it. 'As to worldly knowledge and logical cleverness, I have nothing to do with them; pray let me have a Zen theme.' When this was asked by a monk, the master gave him a hearty blow.

10. The question in which an ancient master's saying is referred to. A monk said to Yün-mên, 'What would one do when no boundaries are seen, however wide the eyes are open?' Said Mên, 'Look!'

11. The question containing words from the sūtras. 'According to the sūtra, all beings are endowed with the Buddha-nature; how is it then that they know it not?' 'They know,' replied Shou-shan.

12. The question containing references to a known fact. 'The ocean is said to contain the precious gem; how can a man lay hands on it?' Replied Fêng-hsüeh: 'When Wang-hsiang comes, its brightness is dazzling; when Li-lou goes, the waves roll as high as the sky. The more one tries to take

F

hold of it, the farther it vanishes; the more one attempts to see it, the darker it grows.'

13. The question that starts from an immediate fact of observation. 'I see that you belong to the Brotherhood, what is the Buddha? What is the Dharma?' San-shêng replied, 'This is the Buddha, this is the Dharma, knowest thou?'

14. The question containing a hypothetical case. 'This Buddha sits in the Hall; what is the other Buddha?' Ching-shan's answer was, 'This Buddha sits in the Hall.'

15. The question embodying a real doubt. 'All things are such as they are from the beginning; what is that which is beyond existence?' 'Your statement is quite plain; what is the use of asking me?' was a master's solution.

16. The question with an aggressive intent. 'The Patriarch came from India and what did he design to do here?' Mu-chou retorted, 'You tell; what did he design?' The monk gave no reply, so Mu-chou struck him.

17. The question plainly and straightforwardly stated. A non-Buddhist philosopher asked the Buddha, 'Words or no-words, I ask neither.' The Buddha remained silent. The philosopher said: 'The Blessed One is indeed full of mercy and compassion. He has cleared off clouds of confusion for my sake, showing me how to enter upon the path.'

18. The question not expressed in words. A non-Buddhist philosopher came to the Buddha and stood before him without uttering a word. The Buddha then said, 'Abundantly indeed, O philosopher!' The philosopher praised him, saying, 'It is all owing to the Blessed One's mercy that I now enter upon the path.'

From this somewhat confused classification we can see how varied were the questions asked and answered among the followers of Zen during the first five hundred years of its steady development after Bodhidharma. Especially is this true during the three hundred years after Hui-nêng, now generally recognized as the sixth patriarch.

8. *The Growth of the Koan System, and its Signification*

No doubt, in these long years of Zen history there was a genuine growth of Zen consciousness among Zen followers, but at the same time, as in everything else, there was a tendency which made for the evaporation of Zen experience into conceptualism. If things were allowed to go on much further in that direction, the genuine experience might entirely die away, and all the literature consisting chiefly of the sayings of the Zen masters would become either unintelligible or a matter of philosophical discussion.

This degeneration, this departure from life and experience, is a phenomenon everywhere observable in the history of religion. There is always in the beginning a creative genius, and a system grows out of his experiences. People of lesser capacity are gathered about him; he endeavours to make them go through the same experiences as his own; he succeeds in some cases, but failures generally exceed successes. Because most of us are not original and creative enough, we are satisfied with following the steps of a leader who appears to us to be so great and so far above. The system thus gradually becomes ossified, and unless there follows a period of revival, the original experiences rapidly die away. In the Chinese history of Zen, this period of decline, we can say, came with the invention of the koan exercise, although it is quite true that this invention was something inevitable in the history of Zen consciousness.

What the koan proposes to do is to develop artificially or systematically in the consciousness of the Zen followers what the early masters produced in themselves spontaneously. It also aspires to develop this Zen experience in a greater number of minds than the master could otherwise hope for. Thus the koan tended to the popularization of Zen and at the same time became the means of conserving the Zen experience in its genuineness. Aristocratic Zen was now turned into a democratic, systematized and, to a certain extent, mechanized Zen. No doubt it meant to that extent a deterioration; but without this innovation Zen might have died out a long time before. To my mind it was the technique of the koan exercise that saved Zen as a unique heritage of Far-Eastern culture.

In order to understand a little better the circumstances which necessitated the rise of koan, let me quote one or two of the masters who lived in the eleventh century. From them we can see that there were at least two tendencies that were at work undermining Zen. They were the doctrine and practice of absolute quietude, and secondly, the habit of intellection that was everywhere impressed upon Zen from the outside. Absolute quietism, which the masters were never tired of combating, was regarded from the outset of Zen history as the essence of Zen teaching; but this tendency, being the inevitable accompaniment of Zen practice, readily and frequently reasserted itself.

As to the intellectual understanding of Zen, the outsiders as well as some Zen advocates are constantly practising it against the experience of Zen. There is no doubt that herein lurks the most deadly enemy of Zen. If they are not effectually put down they are sure to raise their heads again and again, especially when Zen shows any symptoms of decline. Chên-ching K'ê-wên[1] says in one of his sermons: 'As far as Zen is concerned, experience is all in all. Anything not based upon experience is outside Zen. The study of Zen, therefore, must grow out of life itself; and satori must be thoroughly penetrating. If anything is left unexhausted there is an opening to the world of devils.

'Did not an ancient master say that numberless corpses are lying on the smooth, level ground, and also that they are really genuine ones who have passed through thickets of briars and brambles? Nowadays most people are led to imagine that Zen reaches its ultimate end when all the functions of body and mind are suspended, and concentration takes place in one single moment of the present in which

[1] 1024–1102.

a state of eternity-in-one-moment prevails—a state of absolute cessation, a state like an incense-burner in an old roadside shrine, a state of cold aloofness.

'It is most unfortunate that they are unable to realize that this state of concentration, however desirable it may be, when one becomes attached to it hinders the attainment of a true inner perception and the manifestation of the light which is beyond the senses.'

Tai-hui says in a letter to Chên-ju Tao-jên, who was one of his monk disciples: 'There are two forms of error now prevailing among followers of Zen, laymen as well as monks. The one thinks that there are wonderful things hidden in words and phrases, and those who hold this view try to learn many words and phrases. The second goes to the other extreme, forgetting that words are the pointing finger, showing one where to locate the moon. Blindly following the instruction given in the sūtras, where words are said to hinder the right understanding of the truth of Zen and Buddhism, they reject all verbal teachings and simply sit with eyes closed, letting down the eyebrows as if they were completely dead. They call this quiet-sitting, inner contemplation, and silent reflection. Not content with their own solitary practices, they try to induce others also to adopt and practise this wrong view of Zen. To such ignorant and simple-minded followers they would say, "One day of quiet-sitting means one day of progressive striving."

'What a pity! They are not at all aware of the fact that they are planning for a ghostly life. Only when these two erroneous views are done away with is there a chance for real advancement in the mastery of Zen. For we read in the sūtra that while one should not get attached to the artificialities and unrealities which are expressed by all beings through their words and language, neither should one adopt the other view which rejects all words indiscriminately, forgetting that the truth is conveyed in them when they are properly understood, and further, that words and their meanings are neither different nor not different, but are mutually related so that the one without the other is unintelligible. . . .'

There are many other passages expressing similar views in the sayings and discourses of the Zen masters of Tai-hui's day besides those given by him, and from them we can conclude that if Zen were left to its own course, it would surely have degenerated either into the practice of quiet-sitting and silent contemplation, or into the mere memorizing of the many Zen sayings and dialogues. To save the situation and to plan for a further healthy development of Zen, the Zen masters could do nothing better than introduce the innovation of the koan exercises.

What is a koan?

A koan, according to one authority, means 'a public document setting up a standard of judgment', whereby one's Zen understanding is tested as to its correctness. A koan is generally some statement made by an old Zen master, or some answer of his given to a questioner. The following are some that are commonly given to the uninitiated:

1. A monk asked Tung-shan, 'Who is the Buddha?' 'Three *chin* of flax.'

2. Yün-mên was once asked, 'When not a thought is stirring in one's mind, is there any error here?' 'As much as Mount Sumeru.'

3. Chao-chou answered, '*Wu*!' (*mu* in Japanese) to a monk's question, 'Is there Buddha-nature in a dog?' *Wu* literally means 'not' or 'none', but when this is ordinarily given as a koan, it has no reference to its literal signification; it is '*Wu*' pure and simple.

4. When Ming the monk overtook the fugitive Hui-nêng, he wanted Hui-nêng to give up the secret of Zen. Hui-nêng replied, 'What are your original features which you have even prior to your birth?'

5. A monk asked Chao-chou, 'What is the meaning of the First Patriarch's visit to China?' 'The cypress tree in the front courtyard.'

6. When Chao-chou came to study Zen under Nan-ch'üan, he asked, 'What is the Tao (or the Way)?' Nan-ch'üan replied, 'Your everyday mind, that is the Tao.'

7. A monk asked, 'All things are said to be reducible to the One, but where is the One to be reduced?' Chao-chou answered, 'When I was in the district of Ch'ing I had a robe made that weighed seven *chin*.'

8. When P'ang the old Zen adept first came to Ma-tsu in order to master Zen, he asked, 'Who is he who has no companion among the ten thousand things of the world?' Ma-tsu replied, 'When you swallow up in one draught all the water in the Hsi Ch'iang, I will tell you.'

When such problems are given to the uninitiated for solution, what is the object of the master? The idea is to unfold the Zen psychology in the mind of the uninitiated, and to reproduce the state of consciousness, of which these statements are the expression. That is to say, when the koans are understood the master's state of mind is understood, which is satori and without which Zen is a sealed book.

In the beginning of Zen history a question was brought up by the pupil to the notice of the master, who thereby gauged the mental state of the questioner and knew what necessary help to give him. The help thus given was sometimes enough to awaken him to realization, but more frequently than not puzzled and perplexed him beyond description, and the result was an ever-increasing mental strain or 'searching and contriving' on the part of the pupil, of which we have already spoken in the foregoing pages. In actual cases, however, the master would have to wait for a long while for the pupil's first question, if it were coming at all. To ask the first question means more than half the way to its own solution, for it is the outcome of a most intense mental effort for the questioner to bring his mind to a crisis. The question indicates that the crisis is reached and the mind is ready to leave it behind. An experienced master often knows how to lead the pupil to a crisis and to make him successfully pass it. This was really the case before the koan exercise came in vogue, as was already illustrated by the examples of Lin-chi, Nan-yüeh, and others.

As time went on there grew up many 'questions and answers' (*mondō* in Japanese) which were exchanged between masters and pupils. And with the growth of Zen literature it was perfectly natural now for Zen followers to begin to attempt an intellectual solution or interpretation of it. The 'questions and answers' ceased to be experiences and intuitions of Zen consciousness, and became subjects of logical inquiry. This was disastrous, yet inevitable. Therefore the Zen master who wished for the normal development of Zen consciousness and the vigorous growth of Zen tradition would not fail to recognize rightly the actual state of things, and to devise such a method as to achieve finally the attainment of the Zen truth.

The method that would suggest itself in the circumstances was to select some of the statements made by the old masters and to use them as pointers. A pointer would then function in two directions: (1) To check the working of the intellect, or rather to let the intellect see by itself how far it can go, and also that there is a realm into which it as such can never enter; (2) To effect the maturity of Zen consciousness which eventually breaks out into a state of satori.

When the koan works in the first direction there takes place what has been called 'searching and contriving'. Instead of the intellect, which taken by itself forms only a part of our being, the entire personality, mind and body, is thrown out into the solution of the koan. When this extraordinary state of spiritual tension, guided by an experienced master, is made to mature, the koan works itself out into what has been designated as the Zen experience. An intuition of the truth of Zen is now attained, for the wall against which the Yogin has been beating hitherto to no purpose breaks down, and an entirely new vista opens before him. Without the koan the Zen consciousness loses its pointer, and there will never be a state of satori. A psychological *impasse* is the necessary antecedent of satori.

Formerly, that is, before the days of the koan exercise, the antecedent pointer was created in the consciousness of the Yogin by his own intense spirituality. But when Zen became systematized owing to the accumulation of Zen literature in the shape of 'questions and answers' the indispensability of the koan had come to be universally recognized by he masters.

The worst enemy of Zen experience, at least in the beginning, is the intellect, which consists and insists in discriminating subject from object. The discriminating intellect, therefore, must be cut short if Zen consciousness is to unfold itself, and the koan is constructed eminently to serve this end.

On examination we at once notice that there is no room in the koan to insert an intellectual interpretation. The knife is not sharp enough to cut the koan open and see what are its contents. For a koan is not a logical proposition but the expression of a certain mental state resulting from the Zen discipline. For instance, what logical connection can there be between the Buddha and 'three *chin* of flax'? or between the Buddha-nature and '*Wu*'? or between the secret message of Bodhidharma and 'a cypress tree'? In a noted Zen textbook known as *Hekiganshu* (*Pi-yen-chi* in Chinese)[1] Yüan-wu gives the following notes concerning the 'three *chin* of flax', showing how the koan was interpreted by those pseudo-Zen followers who failed to grasp Zen:

'There are some people these days who do not truly understand this koan; this is because there is no crack in it to insert their intellectual teeth. By this I mean that it is altogether too plain and tasteless. Various answers have been given by different masters to the question, "What is the Buddha?" One said, "He sits in the Buddha Hall." Another said, "The one endowed with the thirty-two marks of excellence." Still another, "A bamboo-root whip." None, however, can excel T'ung-shan's "three *chin* of flax" as regards its irrationality, which cuts off all passage of

[1] This is one of the most favourite vademecums of Zen Buddhists. For further explanation see below.

speculation. Some comment that T'ung-shan was weighing flax at the moment, hence the answer. Others say that it was a trick of equivocation on the part of T'ung-shan; and still others think that as the questioner was not conscious of the fact that he was himself the Buddha, T'ung-shan answered him in this indirect way.

'Such [commentators] are all like corpses, for they are utterly unable to comprehend the living truth. There are still others, however, who take the "three *chin* of flax" as the Buddha [thus giving it a pantheistic interpretation]. What wild and fantastic remarks they make! As long as they are beguiled by words, they can never expect to penetrate into the heart of T'ung-shan, even if they live to the time of Maitreya Buddha. Why? Because words are merely a vehicle on which the truth is carried. Not comprehending the meaning of the old master, they endeavour to find it in his words only, but they will find therein nothing to lay their hands on. The truth itself is beyond all description, as is affirmed by an ancient sage, but it is by words that the truth is manifested.

'Let us, then, forget the words when we gain the truth itself. This is done only when we have an insight through experience into that which is indicated by words. The "three *chin* of flax" is like the royal thoroughfare to the capital; when you are once on it every step you take is in the right direction. When Yün-mên was once asked what was the teaching that went beyond the Buddhas and the patriarchs, he said "Dumpling". Yün-mên and T'ung-shan are walking the same road hand in hand. When you are thoroughly cleansed of all the impurities of discrimination, without further ado the truth will be understood. Later the monk who wanted to know what the Buddha was went to Chih-mên and asked him what T'ung-shan meant by "three *chin* of flax". Said Chih-mên, "A mass of flowers, a mass of brocade." He added, "Do you understand?" The monk replied, "No." "Bamboos in the South, trees in the North," was the conclusion of Mên.'

Technically speaking, the koan given to the uninitiated

is intended 'to destroy the root of life', 'to make the calculating mind die', 'to root out the entire mind that has been at work since eternity', etc. This may sound murderous, but the ultimate intent is to go beyond the limits of intellection, and these limits can be crossed over only by exhausting oneself once for all, by using up all the psychic powers at one's command. Logic then turns into psychology, intellection into conation and intuition. What could not be solved on the plane of empirical consciousness is now transferred to the deeper recesses of the mind. So, says a Zen master, 'Unless at one time perspiration has streamed down your back, you cannot see the boat sailing before the wind.' 'Unless once you have been thoroughly drenched in a perspiration you cannot expect to see the revelation of a palace of pearls on a blade of grass.'

The koan refuses to be solved under any easier conditions. But once solved the koan is compared to a piece of brick used to knock at a gate; when the gate is opened the brick is thrown away. The koan is useful as long as the mental doors are closed, but when they are opened it may be forgotten. What one sees after the opening will be something quite unexpected, something that has never before entered even into one's imagination. But when the koan is re-examined from this newly acquired point of view, how marvellously suggestive, how fittingly constructed, although there is nothing artificial here!

9. *Practical Instructions Regarding the Koan Exercise*

The following are some of the practical suggestions that have been given by Zen masters of various ages, regarding the koan exercise; and from them we can gather what a koan is expected to do towards the development of Zen consciousness, and also what tendency the koan exercise has come to manifest as time goes on. As we will see later on, the growth of the koan exercise caused a new movement among the Zen masters of the Ming dynasty to connect it

with the Nembutsu,[1] that is, the recitation of the Buddha-
name. This was owing to the presence of a common
denominator between the psychological mechanism of the
koan exercise and the recitation of the Buddha-name. (The
subject will be given special treatment later on.)

A Zen master of Huang-po Shan, probably of early
Sung, gives the following instruction in the study of Zen:

'O you brother-monks! You may talk glibly and perhaps
intelligently about Zen, about Tao, and scoff at the Buddhas and patriarchs; but when the day comes to reckon up
all your accounts, your lip-Zen will be of no avail. Thus
far you have been beguiling others, but today you will find
that you have been beguiling yourselves. O you brother-
monks! While still strong and healthy in body try to have
real understanding as to what Zen is. After all it is not such
a difficult thing to take hold of the lock; but simply because
you have not made up your minds to die in the last ditch,
if you do not find a way to realization, you say, "It is too
difficult; it is beyond my power." It is absurd! If you are
really men of will, you will find out what your koan means.
A monk once asked Chao-chou, "Has a dog the Buddha-
nature?" to which the master answered, "*Wu!*" Now devote yourselves to this koan and try to find its meaning.
Devote yourselves to it day and night, whether sitting or
lying, whether walking or standing; devote yourselves to
its solution during the entire course of the twelve periods.
Even when dressing or taking meals, or attending to your
natural wants, have your every thought fixed on the koan.
Make resolute efforts to keep it always before your mind.
Days pass, years roll on, but in the fullness of time when
your mind is so attuned and recollected there will be a
sudden awakening within yourselves—an awakening into
the mentality of the Buddhas and the patriarchs. You will
then, for the first time, and wherever you may go, never
again be beguiled by a Zen master.'[2]

---

[1] *Nien-fo*.
[2] From the *Zenkwan Sakushin* ('Breaking Through the Zen Frontier
Gate').

I-an Chên of Fo-chi monastery gives this advice:

'The old saying runs, "When there is enough faith, there is enough doubt which is a great spirit of inquiry, and when there is a great spirit of inquiry there is an illumination." Have everything thoroughly poured out that has accumulated in your mind—learning, hearing, false understanding, clever or witty sayings, the so-called truth of Zen, Buddha's teachings, self-conceit, arrogance, etc. Concentrate yourself on the koan, of which you have not yet had a penetrating comprehension. That is to say, cross your legs firmly, erect your spinal column straight, and paying no attention to the periods of the day, keep up your concentration until you grow unaware of your whereabouts, east, west, south, north, as if you were a living corpse.

'The mind moves in response to the outside world and when it is touched it knows. The time will come when all thoughts cease to stir and there will be no working of consciousness. It is then that all of a sudden you smash your brain to pieces and for the first time realize that the truth is in your own possession from the very beginning. Would not this be great satisfaction to you in your daily life?'

Tai-hui was a great koan advocate of the twelfth century. One of his favourite koans was Chao-chou's 'Wu', but he had also one of his own. He used to carry a short bamboo stick which he held forth before an assembly of monks, and said: 'If you call this a stick, you affirm; if you call it not a stick, you negate. Beyond affirmation and negation what would you call it?' In the following extract from his sermons titled *Tai-hui Pu-shuo*, compiled by T'su-ching, 1190, he gives still another koan to his gardener-monk, Ching-kuang.

'The truth (*dharma*) is not to be mastered by mere seeing, hearing, and thinking. If it is, it is no more than the seeing, hearing, and thinking; it is not at all seeking after the truth itself. For the truth is not in what you hear from others or learn through the understanding. Now keep yourself away from what you have seen, heard, and thought, and see

what you have within yourself. Emptiness only, nothingness, which eludes your grasp and to which you cannot fix
your thought. Why? Because this is the abode where the
senses can never reach. If this abode were within the
reach of your sense it would be something you could
think of, something you could have a glimpse of; it
would then be something subject to the law of birth and
death.

'The main thing is to shut off all your sense-organs and
make your consciousness like a block of wood. When this
block of wood suddenly starts up and makes a noise, that is
the moment you feel like a lion roaming about freely with
nobody disturbing him, or like an elephant that crosses a
stream not minding its swift current. At that moment there
is no fidgeting, nothing doing, just this and no more. Says
P'ing-t'ien the Elder:

> ' "The celestial radiance undimmed,
>   The norm lasting for ever more;
>   For him who entereth this gate,
>   No reasoning, no learning."

'You should know that it is through your seeing, hearing,
and thinking[1] that you enter upon the path, and it is also
through the seeing, hearing, and thinking that you are pre-
vented from entering. Why? Let you be furnished with the
double-bladed sword that destroys and resuscitates life
where you have your seeing, hearing, and thinking, and
you will be able to make good use of the seeing, hearing, and
thinking. But if the sword that cuts both ways, that destroys
as well as resuscitates, is missing, your seeing, hearing, and
thinking will be a great stumbling-block, which will cause
you to prostrate again and again on the ground. Your
truth-eye will be completely blinded; you will be walking
in complete darkness not knowing how to be free and in-

---

[1] (Dṛiṣṭa-śruta-mata-yñāta). Abbreviated for 'the seen, heard, thought
and known'.

dependent. If you want, however, to be the free master of yourself by doing away with your seeing, hearing, and thinking, stop your hankering monkey-like mind from doing mischief; keep it quietly under control; keep your mind firmly collected regardless of what you are doing— sitting or lying, standing or walking, remaining silent or talking; keep your mind like a line stretched taut; do not let it slip out of your hand. Just as soon as it slips out of your control you will find it in the service of the seeing, hearing, and thinking. In such a case is there any remedy? What remedy is applicable here?

'A monk asked Yün-mên, "Who is the Buddha?" "The dried-up dirt-cleaner." This is the remedy; whether you are walking or sitting or lying, let your mind be perpetually fixed on this "dirt-cleaner". The time will come when your mind will suddenly come to a stop like an old rat who finds himself in a *cul-de-sac*. Then there will be a plunging into the unknown with the cry, "Ah, this!" When this cry is uttered you have discovered yourself. You find at the same time that all the teachings of the ancient worthies expounded in the Buddhist Tripitaka, the Taoist Scriptures, and the Confucian Classics, are no more than commentaries upon your own sudden cry, "Ah, this!" '

Tai-hui was never tired of impressing upon his disciples the importance of having satori which goes beyond language and reasoning and which bursts out in one's consciousness by overstepping the limits of consciousness. His letters and sermons are filled with advice and instructions directed towards this end. I quote one or two of them. That he was so insistent on this point proves that Zen in his day was degenerating to a form of mere quietism on the one hand and on the other to the intellectual analysis of the koans left by the old masters.

'The study of Zen must end in satori.[1] It is like a holiday race-boat which is ordinarily put away in some quiet corner, but which is designed for winning a regatta. This has been the case with all the ancient masters of Zen, for

[1] *Wu-ju.*

we know that Zen is really won only when we have satori. You have to have satori somehow, but you will never get what you want by trying to be quiet with yourself, by sitting like a dead man. Why? Does not one of the patriarchs say that when you attempt to gain quietness by suppressing activity your quietness will all the more be susceptible to disturbance? However earnestly you may try to quiet your confused mind, the result will be altogether contrary to what you expect to realize so long as your reasoning habit continues.

'Abandon, therefore, this reasoning habit; have the two characters, "birth" and "death", pasted on your forehead, and fix your attention exclusively on the following koan, as if you were oppressed under the obligation of a very heavy debt. Think of the koan regardless of what you are doing, regardless of what time of the day it is, day or night. A monk asked Chao-chou, "Has a dog the Buddha-nature, or not?" Said Chou, "*Wu!*" Collect your thoughts upon this "*Wu!*" and see what is contained in it. As your concentration goes on you will find the koan altogether devoid of taste, that is, without any intellectual clue whereby to fathom its content. Yet in the meantime you may have a feeling of joy stealing into your heart, which, however, is soon followed by another feeling, this time a feeling of disquietude. Paying no attention to this interweaving of emotions, exert yourself to go ahead with the koan, when you will become aware that you have pushed yourself like the old rat into a blind alley. A turning back will then be necessary, but this can never be accomplished by the weak-minded, who are ever faltering and hesitating.'

In another place Tai-hui says: 'Just steadily go on with your koan every moment of your life. If a thought rises, do not attempt to suppress it by conscious effort; only renew the attempt to keep the koan before the mind. Whether walking or sitting, let your attention be fixed upon it without interruption. When you begin to find it entirely devoid of flavour, the final moment is approaching; do not let it slip out of your grasp. When all of a sudden something flashes out in your mind, its light will illumine the entire universe, and you will see the spiritual land of the Enlightened Ones fully revealed at the point of a single hair, and the great wheel of the Dharma revolving in a single grain of dust.'[1]

K'ung-ku Ching-hung[2] has a similar advice for monks. He says:

'Chao-chou's "*Wu!*", before you have penetrated into its meaning, is like a silver mountain or an iron wall [against which you stand nonplussed]. But as you go on with "*Wu!*" day after day trying to get into its content, and do not give even a moment's rest to yourself, the supreme moment will inevitably come upon you, just as a flood makes its own channel; and then you will see that the iron wall and the silver mountain were not, after all, very formidable. The main point is not to put any reliance on learning, but to put a stop to all hankering, and to exert yourself to the utmost to solve the great problem of birth and death. Do not waste your time by merely thinking of "*Wu!*" as if you were no more than a simpleton, make no attempt to give a false solution to it by means of speculation and imagination. Resolutely put yourself, heart and soul, into the unravelling of the problem of "*Wu!*" When suddenly, as you let go of your hold, there comes a grand overturning of the whole system of consciousness, and for the first time you realize in a most luminous manner what all this finally comes to.'

The author of *The Mirror for Zen Students*[3] confirms all that has already been quoted, and describes fully the psychology of the koan exercise.

---

[1] Tai-hui's passages are taken from a collection of his letters, sermons, discourses, and sayings known as his *Pu-shao*, *Yü-lu*, and *Shu*. He was very well acquainted with the *Avataṁsaka* (or *Gaṇḍavyūha*), and there are many allusions by him to its teachings, as we find in this last sentence here.

[2] Still living in 1466.

[3] Compiled by T'ui-yin, a Korean Zen master of the Ming era (A.D. 1368–1650). The book appeared in 1579.

G

'What is required of Zen devotees is to see into the phrase[1] that liveth and not into the one which is dead. Try to search for the sense of the koan you have, putting your whole mental strength into the task like the mother-hen sitting on her eggs, like a cat trying to catch a rat, like a hungry one eagerly looking everywhere for food, like a thirsty one seeking for water, like a child thinking of its mother. If you exert yourself as seriously and as desperately as that, the time will surely come when the sense of the koan will dawn upon you.

'There are three factors making for success in the study of Zen: (1) great faith, (2) great resolution, and (3) great spirit of inquiry. When any one of these is lacking it is like a cauldron with a broken leg, it limps. At all moments of your life, regardless of what you are doing, exert yourself to see into the meaning of Chao-chou's "*Wu*". Keep the koan always before your mind and never release the spirit of inquiry. As the inquiry goes on steadily and uninter-ruptedly you will come to see that there is no intellectual clue in the koan, that it is altogether devoid of sense as you ordinarily understand that word, that it is entirely flat, devoid of taste, has nothing appetizing about it, and that you are beginning to have a certain feeling of uneasiness and impatience. When you come to this state it is the moment for you to cast aside the scabbard, throw yourself down into the abyss, and by so doing lay a foundation for Buddhahood.

'Do not think that the meaning of the koan is at the moment of your holding it up for solution; do not reason about it or exercise your imagination over it; do not wait for satori to come over you by clearing your mind of its confused ideas; only collect yourself on the unintelligibility

[1] That is, *chü*. The Zen masters generally distinguish two kinds of *chü*; the live one and the dead one. By the 'live *chü*' are meant such statements as give no clues whatever to their rational interpretations but put an end to the functioning of the empirical consciousness; where-as the 'dead *chü*' are those that lend themselves to logical or philosophical treatment and therefore that can be learned from others and committed to memory. This according to T'ui-yin.

of the koan over which the mind evidently has no control.[1] You will finally find yourself like an old rat getting into the furthest corner of the barn where it suddenly perceives by veering clear round the way of escape. To measure the koan by an intellectual standard, as you ordinarily do with other things, to live your life up and down in the stream of birth and death, to be always assailed by feelings of fear, worry, and uncertainty, all this is owing to your imagination and calculating mind. You ought to know how to rise above the trivialities of life, in which most people are found drowning themselves. Do not waste time asking how to do it, just put your whole soul into the business. It is like a mosquito biting at an iron bull; at the very moment the iron absolutely rejects your frail proboscis, you for once forget yourself, you penetrate, and the work is done.'

Sufficient authorities have now been quoted to show where lies the function of the koan in bringing about what is known as satori, and also to show what the Zen master

[1] In some of the Appendices I have given more advice regarding the Zen Yogin's attitude towards the koan, which afford interesting and illuminating materials for the psychological student of Zen consciousness. T'ui-yin cautions his koan students on the following ten points: (1) Do not calculate according to your imagination; (2) Let not your attention be drawn where the master raises his eyebrows or twinkles his eyes; (3) Do not try to extract meaning from the way the koan is worded; (4) Do not try to demonstrate on the words; (5) Do not think that the sense of the koan is to be grasped where it is held out as an object of thought; (6) Do not take Zen for a state of mere passivity; (7) Do not judge the koan with the dualistic standard of *yu* (*asti*) and *wu* (*nāsti*); (8) Do not take the koan as pointing to absolute emptiness; (9) Do not ratiocinate on the koan; and (10) Do not keep your mind in the attitude of waiting for satori to turn up. The koan exercise is confused with so-called meditation, but from all these warnings given by an old master regarding the exercise it is evident that Zen is not an exercise in meditation or in passivity. If Zen is to be properly understood by its students, Eastern and Western, this characteristic aspect of it must be fully comprehended. Zen has its definite object, which is 'to open our minds to satori' as we say, and in order to bring about this state of consciousness a koan is held out before the mental eye, not to meditate on, nor to keep the mind in a state of receptivity, but to use the koan as a kind of pole with which to leap over the stream of relativity to the other side of the Absolute. And the unique feature of Zen Buddhism is that all this is accomplished without resorting to such religious conceptions as sin, faith, God, grace, salvation, a future life, etc.

had in mind when he first began to exercise the minds of his disciples towards the maturing of their Zen consciousness. In the way of summary I conclude this part of the present chapter with a passage from the writings of Hakuin, who is father of the modern Japanese Rinzai school of Zen. In this we will see how the psychology of Zen has been going on without much change for more than a thousand years, since the days of Hui-nêng and his Chinese followers.

'If you want to get at the unadulterated truth of egolessness, you must once for all let go your hold and fall over the precipice, when you will rise again newly awakened and in full possession of the four virtues of eternity, bliss, freedom, and purity, which belong to the real ego. What does it mean to let go of your hold on the precipice? Suppose a man has wandered out among the remote mountains, where no one else has ever ventured. He comes to the edge of a precipice unfathomably deep, the rugged rock covered with moss is extremely slippery, giving him no sure foothold; he can neither advance nor retreat, death is looking at him in the face. His only hope lies in holding on to the vine which his hands have grasped; his very life depends on his holding on to it. If he should by carelessness let go his hold, his body would be thrown down to the abyss and crushed to pieces, bones and all.

'It is the same with the student of Zen. When he grapples with a koan single-handedly he will come to see that he has reached the limit of his mental tension, and he is brought to a standstill. Like the man hanging over the precipice he is completely at a loss what to do next. Except for occasional feelings of uneasiness and despair, it is like death itself. All of a sudden he finds his mind and body wiped out of existence, together with the koan. This is what is known as "letting go your hold". As you become awakened from the stupor and regain your breath it is like drinking water and knowing for yourself that it is cold. It will be a joy inexpressible.'

10. *Various Generalizations on the Koan Exercise*

To recapitulate: The innovation of the koan exercise was inevitable owing to the following circumstances:

1. If the study of Zen had run its natural course it would soon have come to its own extinction owing to the aristocratic nature of its discipline and experience.

2. As Zen gradually exhausted its creative originality in two or three hundred years of development after the time of Hui-nêng, the sixth patriarch, it found that a new life must be awakened in it, if it were to survive, by using some radical method which would vigorously stir up the Zen consciousness.

3. With the passing of the age of creative activity there was an accumulation of materials known as 'stories' (*hua-t'ou*), or 'conditions' (*chi-yüan*), or 'questions and answers' (*mên-ta*), which made up the bulk of Zen history; and this tended to invite intellectual interpretation, ruinous to the maturing of the Zen experience.

4. The rampant growth of Zen quietism since the beginning of Zen history most dangerously threatened the living experience of Zen. The two tendencies, quietism or the school of 'silent illumination', and intuitionalism or the school of noetic experience, had been from the beginning, covertly if not openly, at war with each other.

Because of these conditions, the koan exercise adopted by the Zen masters of the tenth and the eleventh century was designed to perform the following functions:

1. To popularize Zen in order to counteract native aristocracy which tended to its own extinction;

2. To give a new stimulus to the development of Zen consciousness, and thus to accelerate the maturing of the Zen experience;

3. To check the growth of intellectualism in Zen;

4. To save Zen from being buried alive in the darkness of quietism.

From the various quotations which have been given

concerning the koan exercise, the following psychic facts may be gathered:

1. The koan is given to the student first of all to bring about a highly wrought-up state of consciousness.

2. The reasoning faculty is kept in abeyance, that is, the more superficial activity of the mind is set at rest so that its more central and profounder parts which are found generally deeply buried can be brought out and exercised to perform their native functions.

3. The effective and conative centres which are really the foundations of one's personal character are charged to do their utmost in the solution of the koan. This is what the Zen master means when he refers to 'great faith' and 'great spirit of inquiry' as the two most essential powers needed in the qualification of a successful Zen devotee. The fact that all great masters have been willing to give themselves up, body and soul, to the mastery of Zen, proves the greatness of their faith in ultimate reality, and also the strength of their spirit of inquiry known as 'seeking and contriving', which never suspends its activity until it attains its end, that is, until it has come into the very presence of Buddhatā itself.

4. When the mental integration thus reaches its highest mark there obtains a neutral state of consciousness which is erroneously designated as 'ecstasy' by the psychological student of the religious consciousness. This Zen state of consciousness essentially differs from ecstasy in this: Ecstasy is the suspension of the mental powers while the mind is passively engaged in contemplation; the Zen state of consciousness, on the other hand, is the one that has been brought about by the most intensely active exercise of all the fundamental faculties constituting one's personality. They are here positively concentrated on a single object of thought, which is called a state of oneness (*ekāgra*). It is also known as a state of daigi or 'fixation'.[1]

This is the point where the empirical consciousness with all its contents both conscious and unconscious is about to

[1] *Tai-i* in Chinese. First Series, p. 254.

tip over its border-line, and get noetically related to the Unknown, the Beyond, the Unconscious. In ecstasy there is no such tipping or transition, for it is a static finality not permitting further unfoldment. There is nothing in esctasy that corresponds to 'throwing oneself down the precipice', or 'letting go the hold'.

5. Finally, what at first appears to be a temporary suspense of all psychic faculties suddenly becomes charged with new energies hitherto undreamed of. This abrupt transformation has taken place quite frequently by the intrusion of a sound, or a vision, or a form of motor activity. A penetrating insight is born of the inner depths of consciousness, as the source of a new life has been tapped, and with it the koan yields up its secrets.

A philosophical explanation of these psychic facts is offered by Zen Buddhists in the following manner. It goes without saying that Zen is neither psychology nor philosophy, but that it is an experience charged with deep meaning and laden with living, exalting contents. The experience is final and its own authority. It is the ultimate truth, not born of relative knowledge, that gives full satisfaction to all human wants. It must be realized directly within oneself: no outside authorities are to be relied upon. Even the Buddha's teachings and the master's discourses, however deep and true they are, do not belong to one so long as they have not been assimilated into his being, which means that they are to be made to grow directly out of one's own living experiences. This realization is called satori. All koans are the utterances of satori with no intellectual mediations; hence their uncouthness and incomprehensibility.

The Zen master has no deliberate scheme on his part to make his statements of satori uncouth or logically unpalatable; the statements come forth from his inner being, as flowers burst out in spring-time, or as the sun sheds its rays. Therefore to understand them we have to be like flowers or like the sun; we must enter into their inner being. When we reproduce the same psychic conditions out of which the Zen masters have uttered these koans, we shall know them. The masters thus avoid all verbal explanations, which only serve to create in the minds of his disciples an intellectual curiosity to probe into the mystery. The intellect being a most obtrusive hindrance, or rather a deadly enemy, at least in the beginning of Zen study, it must be banished for a while from the mind. The koan is, indeed, a great baffler to reasoning. For this reason, Zen is ever prone to give more value to the psychic facts than to conceptualism. As the facts are directly experienced and prove quite satisfactory, they appeal irresistibly to the 'seeking and contriving' mind of the Zen follower.

As facts of personal experience are valued in Zen, we have such koans as Yün-mên's 'dried up dirt-cleaner,' or Chaochou's 'cypress-tree', T'ung-shan's 'three *chin* of flax', etc., which are all familiar incidents in everyone's life. Compared with the Indian expressions such as 'All is empty, unborn, and beyond causation' or 'The whole universe is contained in one particle of dust', how homely the Chinese are!

Owing to this fact, Zen is better designed to exclude the intellect and to lead our empirical consciousness to its deeper sources. If a noetic experience of a radically different order is to be attained, which sets all our strivings and searchings at rest, something that does not at all belong to the intellectual categories is to be devised. More precisely speaking, something illogical, something irrational, something that does not yield itself to an intellectual treatment is to be the special feature of Zen. The koan exercise was thus the natural development of Zen consciousness in the history of human strivings to reach the ultimate. By means of the koan the entire system of our psychic apparatus is made to bear upon the maturing of the satori state of consciousness.

11. *Personal Records of the Zen Experiences*

Some personal records of the function which is performed by the koan exercise in the maturing of the Zen consciousness are given here. Three of such were already given in the First Series of my *Zen Essays* (pp. 251-258). They are a psychological study by themselves, but my object here is to demonstrate the role of the koan exercise in the practice of Zen and the wisdom of this system as innovated by the Sung masters.

Tê-i of Mêng-shan,[1] who was the eighth descendant of Fa-yen of Wu-tsu Shan (died 1104), tells the following story of his experiences in Zen:

When I was twenty years old I became acquainted with Zen, and before I was thirty-two I had visited seventeen or eighteen Zen masters asking them as to their method of discipline, but none were able to enlighten me on the most important point. When later I came to the master Huan-shan he told me to see into the meaning of '*Wu*' (*mu*), and added, 'Be vigilant over your "*Wu*" through all the periods of the day, as constantly vigilant as a cat is when she tries to catch a rat, or as a hen is while sitting on the eggs. As long as you have as yet no insight, be like a rat gnawing at the coffin-wood and never vacillate in your exertion. As you go on with your task like that, the time will surely come when your mind will become enlightened.'

Following this instruction, I steadily applied myself to the work, day and night. Eighteen days thus elapsed. Suddenly, when I was taking tea, I came upon the meaning of Kāśyapa's smile, which was elicited when the Buddha produced a flower before a congregation of his disciples. I was overjoyed; I wished to find out whether my under-

---

[1] All the quotations cited here are taken from the *Zenkwan Sakushin* ('Aids to Breaking Through the Frontier Gate of Zen'). For the biographical records of these masters see a history of Zen called the *Hui-yüan hsü-liao*.

standing was correct and called upon a few masters of Zen. They, however, gave me no definite answer; some told me to stamp the whole universe with the stamp of Sāgara-mudrā-samādhi, and not to pay attention to anything else. Believing·this, I passed two years. In the sixth month of the fifth year of Ching-ting (1265), I was in Chung-ch'ing, Szŭ-ch'uan, and, suffering a great deal from dysentery, was in a most critical condition. No energy was left in me, nor was the Sāgaramudrā of any avail at this hour. Whatever understanding of Zen I had all failed to support me. The tongue refused to speak, the body to move; all that remained was to greet death. The past unrolled itself before me—the things I had done, as well as the situations I had been in; I was thus in a ghastly state of despondency and completely at a loss as to how to escape from its torture.

At last, determining to be master of myself, I managed to make my will. I then got up quietly, lit some incense, arranged the invalid cushions; I made bows to the Triple Treasure and also to the Nāga gods, and silently confessed my previous sins before them. I prayed that if I were to pass away at this time I might be reborn through the power of Prajñā in a good family and become a monk in my early years. But if I should be cured of this disease I wanted to become a monk at once and devote the rest of my life entirely to the study of Zen. If an illumination should come I would help others even as myself to get enlightened.

After making this prayer, I set up 'Wu' before my mind and turned the light within myself. Before long I felt my viscera twist for a few times, but I paid no attention; it was after some time that my eyelids became rigid and refused to blink, and later on I became unconscious of my own body; the 'Wu' alone occupied my consciousness. In the evening I arose from my seat and found that I was half cured of the disease; I sat down again until the small hours of the morning when the physical disorder completely disappeared. I was myself again, well and in good spirits.

In the eighth month of the same year I went to Chiang-ling and had my head shaved [i.e. became a monk]. Before the year was over, I went on a pilgrimage, and while cooking rice I found out that the koan exercise must be carried on uninterruptedly and with continuous effort. I then settled myself at Huang-lung.

When I felt sleepy for the first time I exercised my will to resist it and kept on sitting, when the sleepiness was easily vanquished. When I became sleepy a second time, I drove it away in a similar manner. A third attack was too strong; I got down from my seat and made bows to the Buddha, which revived me. I resumed my seat and the process had to be repeated. But when at last I had to sleep I used a pillow and slept a little; later my elbow was substituted for the pillow, and finally I altogether avoided lying down. Two nights were thus passed; on the third night I was so fatigued that I felt as if my feet did not touch the ground. Suddenly a dark cloud that seemed to obstruct my vision cleared away, and I felt as if I had just come from a bath and was thoroughly rejuvenated.

As to the koan, a state of mental fixation prevailed, and the koan occupied the centre of attention without any conscious striving on my part for it. All external sensations, the five passions, and the eight disturbances, no longer annoyed me; I was as pure and transparent as a snow-filled silver bowl or as the autumnal sky cleared of all darkening clouds. The exercise thus went on quite successfully but as yet with no turning point.

Later I left this monastery and travelled to Chê. On the way I experienced many hardships and my Zen exercise suffered accordingly. I came to the Ch'êng-t'ien monastery which was presided over by the master Ku-ch'an, and there took up my temporal habitation. I vowed to myself that I would not leave this place until I realized the truth of Zen. In a little over a month I regained what I had lost in the exercise. It was then that my whole body was covered with boils; but I was determined to keep the discipline even at the cost of my life.

This helped a great deal to strengthen my spiritual powers, and I knew how to keep up my seeking and striving (*kung-fu*) even in illness. Being invited out to dinner I walked on with my koan all the way to the devotee's house, but I was so absorbed in my exercise that I passed by the house without even recognizing where I was. This made me realize what was meant by carrying on the exercise even while engaged in active work. My mental condition then was like the reflection of the moon penetrating the depths of a running stream the surface of which was in rapid motion, while the moon itself retained its perfect shape and serenity in spite of the commotion of the water.

On the sixth of the third month I was holding '*Wu*' in my mind as usual while sitting on the cushion, when the head-monk came into the meditation hall. Accidentally he dropped the incense-box on the floor, making a noise. This at once opened my mind to a new spiritual vista, and with a cry I obtained a glimpse into my inner being, capturing the old man Chao-chou [the author of the '*Wu*']. I gave voice to the following extempore stanza:

'Unexpectedly the path comes to an end;
When stamped through, the waves are the water itself.
They say, old Chao-chou stands supremely above the rest,
But nothing extraordinary I find in his features.'

During the autumn I interviewed masters of high reputation such as Hsüeh-yen, T'ui-kêng, Shih-fan, and Hsü-chou. The last-mentioned advised me to go to Huan-shan. When I saw Shan, he asked, 'The light, serenely illuminating, fills all the universe to its furthest limits— are these not the words of the literati Chang-cho?' I was about to open my mouth when Shan gave a '*Ho!*' (*Kwatz!*), and dismissed me unceremoniously. This upset me, and since then my thoughts were concentrated on this attitude of the master. Walking or sitting, eating or drinking, my mind was occupied with it.

Six months passed when, one day in the spring of the following year, I was returning from an out-of-town trip and was about to climb a flight of stone steps, when the

solid ice that had been clogging my brain for so long unexpectedly melted away, and I forgot that I was walking
on the roadway. I immediately went to the master, and
when he repeated his former question I overturned his seat.
I now thoroughly understood the koan, whose knots had
been so hard to untie.

O Brothers! Be thoroughgoing in your Zen exercise.
If I had not been taken ill when at Chung-ch'ing my life
might have been almost wasted. The main thing is to be
introduced to a master with really spiritual insight. Consider how earnestly and steadily the ancient masters devoted themselves both day and night to the study of Zen in
order to grasp the ultimate truth of it.

.   .   .   .   .

Yüan-chon Hsüeh-Yen Tsu-ch'in (died 1287), who was a
disciple of Wu-chou Shih-fan (died 1249), has this to tell
about his experiences:

I left my home when I was five years old, and while
under my master, by listening to his talks to visitors, I began
to know that there was such a thing as Zen, and gradually
came to believe in it, and finally made up my mind to
study it. At sixteen I was ordained as a regular monk and at
eighteen started on a Zen pilgrimage. While staying under
Yüan of Shuang-shan I was kept busy attending to the
affairs of the monastery from morning to evening, and was
never out of the monastery grounds. Even when I was in
the general dormitory or engaged in my own affairs, I kept
my hands folded over my chest and my eyes fixed on the
ground without looking beyond three feet.

My first koan was '*Wu*'. Whenever a thought was stirred
in my mind, I lost no time in keeping it down, and my consciousness was like a cake of solid ice, pure and smooth,
serene and undisturbed. A day passed as rapidly as the
snapping of the fingers. No sound of the bell or the drum
ever reached me.

At nineteen I was staying at the monastery of Ling-yin

when I made the acquaintance of the recorder Lai of
Ch'u-chou. He gave me this advice: 'Your method has no
life in it and will achieve nothing. There is a dualism in it;
you keep movement and quietude as two separate poles of
thought. To exercise yourself properly in Zen you ought to
cherish a spirit of inquiry (*i-ch'ing*); for according to the
strength of your inquiring spirit will be the depth of your
enlightenment.' Thus advised, I had my koan changed to
'the dried-up dirt-wiper'. I began to inquire (*i*) into its
meaning in every possible manner and from every possible
point of view. But being now annoyed by dullness and now
by restlessness, I could not get even a moment of serene
contemplation. I moved to Ching-tzǔ monastery where I
joined a company of seven, all earnest students of Zen.
Sealing up our bedding we determined not to lie down on
the floor. There was a monk called Hsiu who did not join
us, but who kept sitting on his cushion like a solid bar
of iron; I wanted to have a talk with him, but he was
forbidding.

As the practice of not lying down was kept up for two
years I became thoroughly exhausted both in mind and
body. At last I gave myself up to the ordinary way of taking
rest. In two months my health was restored and my spirit
reinvigorated once more by thus yielding to nature. In
fact the study of Zen is not necessarily to be accomplished
by merely practising sleeplessness. It is far better to have
short hours of a sound sleep in the middle of the night when
the mind will gather up fresh energy.

One day I happened to meet Hsiu in the corridor, and
for the first time I could have a talk with him. I asked, 'Why
was it that you avoided me so much last year when I wished
to talk with you?' He said, 'An earnest student of Zen
begrudges even the time to trim his nails; how much more
the time wasted in conversation with others!' I said, 'I am
troubled in two ways, by dullness and restlessness, how can
I get over them?' He replied: 'It is owing to your not being
fully determined in your exercise. Have the cushion high
enough under you, and keeping your spinal column upright,

throw all the spiritual energy you possess into the koan it-self. What is the use of talking about dullness and restless-ness?'

This advice gave me a new turn to my exercise, for in three days and nights I came to realize a state in which the dualism of body and mind ceased to exist. I felt so trans-parent and lively that my eyelids were kept open all the time. On the third day I was walking by the gate still feeling as I did when sitting cross-legged on the cushions. I happened to meet Hsiu, who asked, 'What are you doing here?' I answered, 'Trying to realize the truth (*tao*).' 'What do you mean by the truth?' he asked. I could not give him a reply, which only increased my mental annoyance.

Wishing to return to the meditation hall I directed my steps towards it, when I encountered the head-monk. He said, 'Keep your eyes wide open and see what it all means.' This encouraged me. I came back into the hall and was about to go to my seat when the whole outlook changed. A broad expanse opened, and the ground appeared as if all caved in. The experience was beyond description and alto-gether incommunicable, for there was nothing in the world to which it could be compared. Coming down from the seat I sought Hsiu. He was greatly pleased, and kept repeating: 'How glad I am! How glad I am!' We took hold of each other's hands and walked along the willow embankment outside the gate. As I looked around and up and down, the whole universe with its multitudinous sense-objects now appeared quite different; what was loathsome before, together with ignorance and passions, was now seen to be nothing else but the outflow of my own inmost nature which in itself remained bright, true, and transparent. This state of consciousness lasted for more than half a month.

Unfortunately, as I did not happen to interview a great master of deeper spiritual insight at the time, I was left at this stage of enlightenment for some time. It was still an imperfect stage which if adhered to as final would have obstructed the growth of a truly penetrating insight; the sleeping and waking hours did not yet coalesce into a unity. Koans that admitted some way of reasoning were intelligible enough, but those that altogether defied it, as if they were a wall of iron blocks, were still quite beyond my reach. I passed many years under the master Wu-chun, listening to his sermons and asking his advice, but there was no word which gave a final solution to my inner disquietude, nor was there anything in the sūtras or the sayings of the masters, as far as I read, that could cure me of this heartache.

Ten years thus passed without my being able to remove this hard inner obstruction. One day I was walking in the Buddha Hall at T'ien-mu when my eyes happened to fall on an old cypress-tree outside the Hall. Just seeing this old tree opened a new spiritual vista and the solid mass of obstruction suddenly dissolved. It was as if I had come into the bright sunshine after having been shut up in the darkness. After this I entertained no further doubt regarding life, death, the Buddha, or the Patriarchs. I now realized for the first time what constituted the inner life of my master Wu-chun, who indeed deserved thirty hard blows.

T'ien-shan Ch'iung, who was disciple of Tê-i of Mêng-shan, has the following to record:

When I was thirteen years old I came to know something about Buddhism; at eighteen I left home and at twenty-two was ordained a monk. I first went to Shih-chuang where I learned that the monk Hsiang used to look at the top of his nose all the time and that this kept his mind transparent. Later, a monk brought from Hsüeh-yen his 'Advice Regarding the Practice of Meditation (za-zen)'. By this I found that my practice was on a wrong track. So I went to Hsüeh-yen, and following his instructions exercised myself exclusively on 'Wu'. On the fourth night I found myself perspiring, but my mind was clear and lucid. While in the Hall I never conversed with others, wholly devoting myself to zazen.

Later on I went to the master Miao of Kao-fêng, who

said this to me: 'Let there be no intermission in your exercise during the twelve periods of the day. Get up in the small hours of the morning and seek out your koan at once so that it will be held all the time before you. When you feel tired and sleepy, rise from your seat and walk the floor, but even while walking do not let your koan slip away from your mind. Whether you are eating, or working, or engaged in monastery affairs, never fail to keep your koan before you. When this is done by day and night, a state of oneness will prevail, and later your mind will surely open to enlightenment.' I then kept up my exercise according to this advice, and surely enough I finally achieved a state of oneness. On the twentieth of March Yen gave me a sermon to this effect:

'Brethren, when you feel too drowsy after a long sitting on the cushions, come down on the floor, have a run around the hall, rinse your mouth, and bathe your face and eyes with cold water; after that resume your sitting on the cushions. Keeping your spinal column straight up like an outstanding precipice, throw all your mental energy on the koan. If you go on like this for seven days, I can assure you of your coming to enlightenment, for this is what happened to me forty years ago.'

I followed this advice and found my exercise gaining more light and strength than usual. On the second day I could not close my eyelids even if I wanted to; on the third day I felt as if I were walking in the air; and on the fourth day all worldly affairs ceased to bother me. That night I was leaning against the railing for a while, and when I examined myself I found that the field of consciousness seemed to be all empty, except for the presence of the koan itself. I turned around and sat on the cushion again, when all of a sudden I felt as if my whole body from head to foot were split like a skull; I felt as if I were taken out of an abysmal depth and thrown up into the air. My joy knew no bounds!

My experience was presented to Yen, but it did not meet his full approval. He advised me to go on with my exercise

H

as before. When I asked for further instruction, among other things he gave me this: 'If you really wish to attain the highest truth of Buddhism, there is still something lacking in your understanding, there ought to be a really final stroke. Say to yourself, "Where do I lack this finality?" I could not believe his words, and yet there was a shadow of doubt lurking in my mind. So I went on stolidly with my zazen every day as before for about six months more.

One day I had a headache and was preparing a medicine when a monk known as Chiao the Red-nosed asked me how I understood the story of Prince Nata?[1]

Thus asked, I remembered that I was once asked by the senior monk Wu about the same story, but failed to give him a reply. This remembrance at once led to the solution.

Later on, after Yen had passed away, I went to Mêng-shan, and Shan asked, 'Where in the study of Zen do you consider yourself to have reached its consummation?' I did not know what to say. Shan then told me to exercise myself in tranquillization so that all the dust of worldliness might be thoroughly removed. But whenever I entered his room and tried to say a word he at once remarked, 'Something lacking.' One day I began my zazen at four in the afternoon and continued until four in the morning, and through sheer power of concentration I reached an exquisite state of ecstasy. Coming out of it I saw the master and told him about it. He then asked, 'What is your original self?' I was about to speak when he shut the door in my face.

After this I exerted myself more and more in zazen and was able to experience many exquisite states of mind. Though I had to see my former master pass away before I had penetrated into the details of Zen, yet fortunately

[1] 'Prince Nata rending himself asunder gives his flesh back to his mother and his bones to his father and then manifesting his own original body and by his miraculous powers preaches the Dharma for the benefit of his parents.' This is one of the well-known koans. The idea is to make the student interview this 'original body' shorn of all its trappings, physical, mental, or spiritual.

through the guidance of the present master I have been led into deeper realizations. In truth, when one is earnest and resolute enough, realizations will come to one frequently and there will be a stripping-off at each step forward.

One day when I was looking at the 'Inscriptions'[1] by the third patriarch, in which I read, 'When one returns to the root, the meaning is realized, but when one follows only the appearance, the substance is lost', then there was another stripping-off. The master Shan said: 'The study of Zen is like the polishing of a gem; the more polished the brighter the gem, and when it becomes thus brighter, let it still be polished up. When there is the more stripping-off of its outer coatings, this life of yours will grow worth more than a gem.'

But whenever I attempted to utter a word, the master would at once declare, 'Something lacking.' One day when deeply absorbed in meditation, I came across this 'something lacking'. All the bonds that had hitherto bound my mind and body were dissolved at once, together with every piece of my bones and their marrow. It was like seeing the sun suddenly bursting through the snow-laden clouds and brightly shining. As I could not contain myself, I jumped down at once from the seat, and running to the master took hold of him, exclaiming, 'Now, what am I lacking?' He gave me three slaps and I bowed to him profoundly. Said the master, 'O T'ien-shan, for many years you have exerted yourself for this very thing. Today, at last, you have it.'

Wu-wên T'sung of Hsiang-shan succeeded Ch'ing as a Zen master, and the following is his Zen experience:

Tu-wêng was the first master I saw in my study of Zen; he had me inquire into the meaning of 'Neither mind, nor Buddha, nor a thing, this.' Later we formed a group of six including Yün-fêng and Yüeh-shan, so that we might be a stimulation to one another in the Zen exercise. Next I saw the master Chiao Wu-nêng, who gave me 'Wu!' Next I went

[1] The First Series, p. 196.

to Chang-lu where, again, I had friends together in order to encourage one another. I happened to meet the brother-monk Ching of Huai-shan, who asked, 'What is your understanding of Zen after several years of study?' I replied, 'Not a thought stirring all day.' Ching asked further, 'Where does this notion of yours originate?' I felt as if I knew but I was not quite sure how to answer him. Seeing that I had no insight into the gist of the matter, Ching told me that I was all right as far as my tranquillization went, but that I had no hold of the thing in its activity. This surprised me and I begged him to advise me as to how my exercise should be carried on so as to have an insight into the matter. Said Ching: 'Don't you know what Ch'uan-lao says? "If one wants to have an understanding in the matter, look at the North Star by turning around towards the south",' and without making further remarks he went away.

Thus questioned, I did not know what to say. Whether walking or sitting my mind refused to dwell on anything else, and for several succeeding days 'Wu', was dropped and this 'North Star seen in the south' occupied my attention exclusively. One day I found myself in the shaving-room where I was sitting with others on a block of wood; the 'doubt' (i) firmly took hold of me and time passed without my knowing, and it was about meal time when without premonition I felt my mind broadening out, becoming clear, light, and serene. It seemed my whole mental system was broken up and its coatings were all stripped off; the entire world with all its objects, sentient and non-sentient, vanished before me; and there was a vast vacuity.

After a while I was awakened, feeling perspiration running down my whole body, and I knew what was meant by seeing the North Star in the south. I met Ching, and he asked, 'Who is it that comes this way?' I replied, 'Neither the self nor the other.' He said, 'If it is neither the self nor the other, what is it after all?' 'One who eats when hungry and sleeps when tired out,' I answered. Ching then made me express the experience in verse, which I did, and everything went on with no impediment. But still there was something final, and I was impressed that I had not yet grasped it.

Later on, I went into the mountains of Hsiang-yen where I passed the summer. The mosquitoes were terrible and I could not keep my hands in position. Then I thought of the ancient masters who had sacrificed their very lives for the sake of the Dharma—why then should I be bothered by mosquitoes? I made up my mind not to be disturbed by them any longer. Firmly setting my teeth, clenching my fists, I held up the '*Wu*' before me and made a most desperate fight against the insects. While I was thus subjecting myself to a test of endurance it so happened that my body and mind finally attained a state of quietude. It felt as if the whole building with all its walls had crashed down leaving me in a vast void—an experience which nothing earthly could describe. My sitting lasted from about seven in the morning until two in the afternoon. I then realized that Buddhism contains the whole truth and that it is altogether due to our not being thorough enough in the attempt to grasp it that we sometimes imagine Buddhism to be misleading.

While my understanding of Zen was clear and full, there was yet something not quite thoroughly exhausted in the hidden and almost inapproachable recesses of my consciousness; so I retired again into the mountains for six years in Kwang-chou, for another six years in Li-an, and finally for three years again in Kwang-chou, when I was released in the fullest sense of the term.

12. *The Importance and the Function of the Spirit of Inquiry*

As has already been stated, the preparatory equipment of the Zen devotee before he takes up the koan exercise is:

1. To awaken a most sincere desire to be delivered from the bondage of karma, from the pain of birth and death;

2. To recognize that the aim of the Buddhist life consists

in attaining enlightenment, in maturing a state of consciousness known as satori;

3. To realize the futility of all intellectual attempts to
reach this aim, that is, to solve in a most living manner the
ultimate problem of existence;

4. To believe that the realization of satori means the
awakening of Buddhatā which lies deeply buried in all
minds;

5. To be in possession of a strong spirit of inquiry which
will ever urge a man to experience within himself the presence of Buddhatā. Without this fivefold equipment he may
not hope to carry out the koan exercise successfully to its end.

Even when he is thus mentally qualified, he may not
believe the koan to be the most efficient means to reach the
goal. It may be that he is more attracted to the Shingon or
T'ien-tai method of discipline, or to the recitation of the
Buddha's name as in the Pure Land sects, or to the repetition of the Daimoku as in the Nichiren sect. This is where
what may be termed his religious idiosyncrasies rule, which
are due to his previous karma. In this case, he cannot be a
successful follower of Zen, and his emancipation will have
to be effected in some other way.

Even among Zen followers there are some who are no
believers in the koan, regarding it as something artificially
contrived; indeed, they even go further and declare satori
itself to be a sort of excrescence which does not properly
belong to the original system of Zen. Most Japanese
adherents of the Sōtō school of Zen belong to this class of
koan denouncers. This divergence of views as to the efficacy
of the koan exercise and the experience of satori comes
rather from the differences of philosophical interpretation
given to Zen by the followers of the Sōtō and the Rinzai.
As far as the practice of Zen is concerned, both the Sōtō and
the Rinzai are descendants of Bodhidharma and Hui-nêng.

However this may be, one must believe in the koan if
he is to disciplined in it and awakened by it to satori. Now
the question is: How is a koan—at least the first koan—to
be brought up into the field of consciousness so as to occupy

its centre when one undertakes to solve its meaning? It evidently has no logical connotation, for its express purpose is to cut off every passage to speculation and imagination. For instance, when '*Wu*' or '*Mu*' is given to a Zen Yogin, how is he expected to deal with it? There is no doubt that he is not to think about it, for no logical thinking is possible. '*Wu*' does not yield any meaning inasmuch as it is not to be thought of in connection with the dog, nor for that matter with the Buddha-nature, either; it is '*Wu*' pure and simple. The koan neither denies nor asserts the presence of Buddha-nature in the dog, although Chao-chou used the '*Wu*' on being asked about the Buddha-nature. When the '*Wu*' is given as a koan to the uninitiated, it stands by itself; and this is exactly what is claimed from the beginning by Zen masters, who have used it as an eye-opener.

So with 'the Cypress-tree'. It is simply 'the Cypress-tree', and has no logical connection with the question: 'What is the idea of the First Patriarch's visit to China?' Nor does it at all refer to the pantheistic view of existence, which is sometimes thought to be the world-conception of the Buddhists. This being the case, what mental attitude shall we take to the koan when it is given us as the key to the secrets of Zen?

Generally, the Chinese characters used in describing the mental attitude towards a koan are: *t'i-ch'i, t'i-szŭ, t'i-to, chu*, meaning, 'to lift', 'to hold up', 'to raise'; *k'an*, 'to see', 'to regard', 'to hold before the eye'; *san*, 'to be concerned with', 'to be in', 'to consult', 'to refer to'; *san-chiu* or *t'i-chiu*, 'to investigate', 'to inquire into'; *kung-fu*, 'to seek a clue', 'to search for a solution', 'to exercise one's mind on a subject'; *yai*, to 'examine'. All these terms purport to mean 'to keep a koan continually before one's mental eye so as to make one endeavour to find a clue to its secrets'.

These two processes, the holding up and the striving, may be considered one; for the sole object of holding up a koan before the mind is to see into its meaning. As this goes on, the meaning searched after objectively in '*Wu*', 'Cypress-tree', or 'three *chin* of flax', exfoliates itself, not from the koan indeed, but from within the Yogin's own mind. This is the moment when the koan becomes perfectly identified with the searching and striving mind, and the meaning yields itself through this identification.

It may not thus be proper to say that the koan is understood, for at the moment of understanding there is no koan separate from the mind. Nor is it proper to assert that it is the mind that understands itself, for the understanding is a reflection, an aftermath; a mind is the reconstruction of the understanding. There is as yet no judgment here, no subject, no predicate; there is simply the exclamation, 'Ah!' The Chinese terms used in this connection are quite graphic: *hê ti i hsia* or *p'ên ti i fa*, which means 'one outbursting cry'. The moment is thus: 'the bursting of the bag', 'the breaking up of the tar-casket', 'a sudden snapping', 'a sudden bursting', 'the bursting of the bamboo with a crack', 'the breaking up of the void', etc.

The word 'concentration' has been used very much in the koan exercise; but, in fact, concentration is not the main point, though it inevitably follows. The thing most essential in the exercise is the will to get into the meaning—we have at present no suitable expression—of the koan. When the will or the spirit of inquiry is strong and constantly working, the koan is necessarily kept without interruption before the eye, and all the other thoughts that are not at all cogent are naturally swept off the field of consciousness. This exclusion and sweeping off is a byproduct, it is more or less accidental. This is where the koan exercise is distinct from mere concentration and also from the Indian form of Dhyāna, that is, meditation, abstraction, or thought-cessation.

Two forms of concentration may be distinguished now; the one brought about as it were mechanically, and the other resulting inevitably, but in essence accidentally, from the intensification of an inquiring spirit. When concentration followed by identification is once attained either way, it necessarily ends in the final outburst of satori. But genuine Zen always requires the presence of a spirit of inquiry, as is shown in the following quotations.

Tai-hui, who was one of the earlier advocates of the koan, was always emphatic about this point; for we find references to it everywhere in his discourses known as *Tai-hui's Sermons*.[1] Consider such statements as the following: 'Single out the point where you have been in doubt all your life and put it upon your forehead.' 'Is it a holy one, or a commonplace one? Is it an entity, or a non-entity? Press your question to its very end. Do not be afraid of plunging yourself into a vacuity: find out what it is that cherishes the sense of fear. Is it a void, or is it not?'

Tai-hui never advises us just to hold up a koan before the mind; he tells us, on the contrary, to make it occupy the very centre of attention by the sheer strength of an inquiring spirit. When a koan is backed up by such a spirit, it is, he says, 'like a great consuming fire which burns up every insect of idle speculation that approaches it'. Without this stimulating spirit of inquiry philosophically coloured, no koan can be made to hold up its position before the consciousness. Therefore, it is almost a common-sense saying among Zen masters to declare that, 'In the mastery of Zen the most important thing is to keep up a spirit of inquiry; the stronger the spirit the greater will be the satori that follows; there is, indeed, no satori when there is no spirit of inquiry; therefore begin by inquiring into the meaning of a koan.'

According to Kao-fêng Yüan-miao,[2] we have this:

'The koan I ordinarily give to my pupils is: "All things return to the One; where does the One return?" I make them search after this. To search after it means to awaken a great inquiring spirit for the ultimate meaning of the koan. The multitudinousness of things is reducible to the One, but where does this One finally return? I say to them: Make this inquiry with all the strength that lies in your personality, giving yourself no time to relax in this effort. In whatever physical position you are, and in whatever business you are employed, never pass your time idly. Where

---

[1] *Tai-hui p'u-shuo.*
[2] 1238–1295.

does the One finally return? Try to get a definite answer to this query. Do not give yourself up to a state of doing nothing; do not exercise your fantastic imagination, but try to bring about a state of perfect identification by pressing your spirit of inquiry forward, steadily and uninterruptedly. You will be then like a person who is critically ill, having no appetite for what you eat or drink. Again you will be like an idiot, with no knowledge of what is what. When your searching spirit comes to this stage, the time has come for your mental flower to burst out.'

Ku-yin Ching-ch'in, late in the fifteenth century, has this to say regarding the koan exercise:

' "Searching and contriving" (kung-fu) may best be practised where noise and confusion do not reach; cut yourself off from all disturbing conditions; put a stop to speculation and imagination; and apply yourself whole-heartedly to the task of holding on to your koan, never letting it go off the centre of consciousness, whether you are sitting or lying, walking or standing still. Never mind in what condition you are placed, whether pleasing or dis-agreeable, but try all the time to keep the koan in mind, and reflect within yourself who it is that is pursuing the koan so untiringly and asking you this question so unremittingly.

'As you thus go on, intensely in earnest, inquiring after the inquirer himself, the time will most assuredly come to you when it is absolutely impossible for you to go on with your inquiry, as if you had come to the very fountain of a stream and were blocked by the mountains all around. This is the time when the tree together with the entwining wistaria breaks down, that is, when the distinction of sub-ject and object is utterly obliterated, when the inquiring and the inquired are fused into one perfect identity. Awakening from this identification, there takes place a great satori that brings peace to all your inquiries and searchings.'

T'ien-ch'i Shui's[1] advice to students of Zen is this:

'Have your minds thoroughly washed off of all cunning and crookedness, sever yourselves from greed and anger which

[1] From Chu-hung's *Biographies of the Famous Zen Masters of Ming*.

rise from egotism, and let no dualistic thoughts disturb you any longer so that your consciousness is wiped perfectly clean. When this purgation is effected, hold up your koan before the mind: "All things are resolvable into the One, and when is this One resolved? Where is it really ultimately resolved?"

'Inquire into this problem from beginning to end, severally as so many queries, or undividedly as one piece of thought, or simply inquire into the whereabouts of the One. In any event, let the whole string of questions be distinctly impressed upon your consciousness so as to make it the exclusive object of attention. If you allow any idle thought to enter into the one solid uninterruptible chain of inquiries, the outcome will ruin the whole exercise.

'When you have no koan to be held before your minds, there will be no occasion for you to realize a state of satori. To seek satori without a koan is like boiling sands which will never yield nourishing rice.

'The first essential thing is to awaken a great spirit of inquiry and strive to see where the One finally resolves itself. When this spirit is kept constantly alive so that no chance is given to languor or heaviness or otioseness to assert itself, the time will come to you without your specially seeking it when the mind attains a state of perfect concentration. That is to say, when you are sitting, you are not conscious of the fact; so with your walking or lying or standing, you are not at all conscious of what you are doing; nor are you aware of your whereabouts, east or west, south or north; you forget that you are in possession of the six senses; the day is like the night, and *vice versa*. But this is still midway to satori, and surely not satori itself. You will have yet to make another final and decided effort to break through this, a state of ecstasy, when the vacuity of space will be smashed to pieces and all things reduced to perfect evenness. It is again like the sun revealing itself from behind the clouds, when things worldly and super-worldly present themselves in perfect objectivity.'

According to Ch'u-shan Shao-ch'i:[1]

[1] Chu-hung's *Biographies*.

'It is necessary for the uninitiated to have a kind of too wherewith to take hold of Zen; and it is for this reason that they are told to practise the Nembutsu, that is, to be thinking of the Buddha. The Buddha is no other than Mind, or rather, that which desires to see this Mind. Where does this desire, this thought, take its rise? From the Mind, we all say. And this Mind is neither a mind, nor a Buddha, nor a something. What is it then?

'To find it out, let them abandon all that they have accumulated in the way of learning, intellection, and knowledge; and let them devote themselves exclusively to this one question, "Who is it that practises the Nembutsu (*namu-amida-butsu*)?" Let this inquiring spirit assert itself to the highest degree. Do not try to reason it out; do not assume a state of mere passivity for satori to come by itself; do not allow yourself to cherish false thoughts and imaginations; do not let ideas of discrimination assert themselves. When your striving and seeking is constant, permitting no breaks and interruptions, your Dhyāna will naturally be matured, and your inquiring spirit (*i-t'uan*) brought up to the inevitable crisis. You will then see that Nirvāṇa and Saṁsāra, the land of purity and the land of defilement, are mere idle talk, and that there is from the beginning nothing requiring explanation or commentary, and further that Mind is not a somewhat belonging to the realm of empirical consciousness and therefore not an object of mental comprehension.'[1]

Tu-fêng Chi-shan,[2] who flourished in the latter half of the fifteenth century, used to advocate strongly the awakening of an inquiring spirit, as is seen in the following passage :[3]

[1] *Pu-k'ê-tê, anupalabdha* in Sanskrit.
[2] His stanza on the Zen experience is recorded in Chu-hung's *Biographies of the Famous Zen Masters of Ming*:
    'Here rules an absolute quietness, all doings subside;
    Just a touch, and lo, a roaring thunder-clap!
    A noise that shakes the earth, and all silence;
    The skull is broken to pieces, and awakened I am from the
        dream!'
[3] Quoted in the *Ch'an-kuan ts'ê-chin* ('Aids to Breaking Through the Frontier Gate of Zen').

'If you are determined to escape birth and death, a great believing heart is first of all to be awakened and great vows to be established. Let this be your prayer: So long as the koan I am holding this moment is not solved, so long as my own face which I have even prior to my birth is not seen, so long as the subtle deeds of transmigration are not destroyed, I make up my mind most resolutely not to abandon the koan given me for solution, not to keep myself away from truly wise teachers, and not to become a greedy pursuer of fame and wealth; and when these determinations are deliberately violated, may I fall in the evil paths. Establishing this vow, keep a steady watch over your heart so that you will be a worthy recipient of a koan.

'When you are told to see into the meaning of "*Wu*" the essential thing to do in this case is to let your thought be focussed on the "why" of the Buddha-nature being absent in the dog. When the koan deals with the oneness of all things, let your thought be fixed on the "where" of this oneness. When you are told to inquire into the sense of the Nembutsu, let your attention be principally drawn on the "who" of the Nembutsu. Thus, turning your light of reflection inwardly, endeavour to enter deeply into a spirit of inquiry. If you feel that you are not gaining strength in this exercise, repeat the whole koan as one complete piece of statement from the beginning to the end. This orderly pursuance of the koan will help you to raise your spirit of inquiry as to the outcome of it. When this spirit is kept alive without interruption and most sincerely, the time will come to you when you perform, even without being aware of it, a somersault in the air. After experiencing this you may come back to me and see how my blows are dealt out.'

K'ung-ku Lung[1] seems to be an advocate of the Nembutsu as well as the koan, but as far as he advises his pupils to exercise themselves on a koan, he upholds the spirit of inquiry to be the sustaining force in the exercise. For he says that the koan is to be 'silently inquired into' (*mo-mo t'san chiu*), that the '*Wu*' is to be 'made lucid' (*ming*) by

[1] From Chu-hung's *Biographies*.

'furiously' (*fên-fên-jan*) attending to it; that students of Zen should apply themselves to this thought, 'This mind is kept working while the body continues its Māyā-like existence, but where is it to rest when the dead body is cremated?' To find out where the oneness of things ultimately lies, the student must reflect within himself and inquire into the problem so as to locate definitely its whereabouts.[1]

All these masters belonging to late Yüan and early Ming, when the koan system became a definitely settled method in the mastery of Zen, agree in keeping up a strong inquiring spirit as regards the meaning of the koan or the spirit itself that thus inquires. The koan is not just to be held up before the mind as something that gathers up like a magnet all one's mental energies about it; the holding must be sustained and nourished by the strong undercurrent of spiritual energy without whose backing the holding becomes mechanical and Zen loses its creative vitality.

We may question: Why is not the mechanical method also in full accord with the spirit of Zen? Why is the inquiring method to be preferred? Why is it necessary to keep up the spirit of inquiry throughout the koan exercise? Has it anything to do with the nature of satori itself that emerges from the exercise? The reason why the masters have all emphasized the importance of the inquiring spirit is, in my view, owing to the fact that the koan exercise started first to reproduce the Zen consciousness, which had grown up naturally in the minds of the earlier Zen devotees. Before these earlier men had taken to the study of Zen, they were invariably good students of Buddhist philosophy; indeed, they were so well versed in it that they finally became dissatisfied with it; for they came to realize that there was something deeper in its teachings than mere

---

[1] Chu-hung comments on Lung's view of the Nembutsu: When the question is concerned with the Nembutsu, Lung is not so particular about cherishing a spirit of inquiry as was generally done in his day. For he states in one of his letters that while, according to the master Yu-t'an, one is advised to inquire into the 'who' of the Nembutsu, this inquiring form of Nembutsu is not absolutely necessary, for just to practise it in one's ordinary frame of mind will be enough.

analysis and intellectual comprehension. The desire to penetrate behind the screen was quite strong in them.

What is the Mind, or the Buddhatā, or the Unconscious that is always posited behind the multitudinousness of things, and that is felt to be within ourselves? They desired to grasp it directly, intuitively, as the Buddhas of the past had all done. Impelled by this desire to know, which is the spirit of inquiry, they reflected within themselves so intensely, so constantly, that the gate was finally opened to them, and they understood. This constant knocking at the gate was the antecedent condition that always seemed to be present and that resulted in the maturing of their Zen consciousness.

The object of the Zen exercise is to bring about this intense state of consciousness, in a sense artificially, for the masters could not wait for a Zen genius to rise spontaneously,[1] and therefore sporadically, from among their less spiritually-equipped brothers. Unless the aristocratic nature of Zen was somewhat moderated, so that even men of ordinary capacity could live the life of a Zen master, Zen itself might rapidly disappear from the land where Bodhidharma and his followers had taken such special pains to make its root strike in deeply. Zen was to be democratized, that is, systematized.

Pao-nêng Jên-yang[2] says in one of his sermons: 'Should-

---

[1] According to Kung-ku Lung: 'Anciently, there were probably some who had satori without resorting to the koan exercise, but there are none nowadays who can ever attain satori without strenuously applying themselves to the exercise.'

[2] Pao-nêng Jên-yang was a disciple of Yang-ch'i Fang-hui (died 1046). Before he became a Zen devotee he was a great scholar of T'ien-tai philosophy. When he came to Hsüeh-tou, who was a great figure in the Yün-mên school of Zen, the master at once recognized in him a future Zen master. To stimulate him, Hsüeh-tou addressed him sarcastically, 'O you great college professor!' The remark stung Jên-yang to the quick, and he determined to surpass in Zen even this great master. When he finally became a master himself, as Hsüeh-tou had expected, he once appeared in the pulpit and said: 'Behold, I am now in the tongue-pulling hell!' So saying, he was seen as if pulling out his tongue with his own hand and exclaimed: 'Oh! Oh! This hell is meant for liars.' Another time, seeing his attendant-monk offering incense to the Buddha, preparatory for a regular discourse to be given by the master, he said, 'Monks, my attendant has already given you a sermon,' and without another word he came down from the pulpit.

ering a bag, holding a bowl, I have been pilgrimaging for more than twenty years all over the country and visited more than a dozen masters of Zen. But at present I have no special attainment to call my own. If I have, I can tell you, I am not much better than a piece of rock devoid of intelligence. Nor had those reverend masters of Zen whom I visited any special attainment which might benefit others. Ever since I remain a perfect ignoramus with no knowledge of anything, with no intelligence to understand anything. I am, however, satisfied with myself. Inadvertently carried by the wind of karma I find myself at present in the country of Chiang-nêng, and have been made to preside over this humble monastery and to lead others, mixing myself with people of the world. Here thus as a host I serve all the pilgrims coming from various parts of the country. There is enough of salt, sauce, porridge, and rice with which to feed them sufficiently. My time, thus engaged, is passed quietly, but as to the truth of Buddhism there is not even a shadow of it to dream of.'

If all Zen masters held themselves on to this exalted view of Zen Buddhism, who would ever be able to succeed them and uninterruptedly transmit to posterity their experience and teaching?

Shih-t'ien Fa-hsün (1170–1244) says:[1]

'Very few indeed there are who can walk the path of our
    Fathers!
In depth and steepness it surpasses an abysmal pit;
Uselessly I extend the hand to help the passengers;
Let the moss in my front court grow as green as it chooses.'

This view of Zen is what we must expect of course of a genuine Zen master, but when the moss of the Zen courtyard is never disturbed by the footsteps of any human beings, what will become of Zen? The path must be made walkable, to a certain extent at least; some artificial means

[1] From his *Sayings*, Vol. II.

must be devised to attract some minds who may one day turn out to be true transmitters of Zen.[1]

The rise of the koan exercise was altogether a natural growth in the history of Zen. Being so, the function of a first koan must be to reproduce as it were artificially the same state of consciousness that was experienced by the earlier masters in a more spontaneous way. This means to bring the spirit of inquiry into a point of concentration or 'fixation'. The koan shows no logical clue to take hold of in an intellectual and discursive manner, and therefore an uninitiated Yogin has to turn away from logic to psychology, from ideation to personal experience, from what is his own only superficially to his inmost being.

The koan does not, indeed, make light of reasoning, that is, it does not try to check it by force; but as the koan stands before the Yogin like 'an iron wall and a silver mountain' against any advance of speculation or imagination, he has no choice but to abandon reasoning. He must find some other means of approach. He cannot yield up his spirit of inquiry, for it is that which makes him stronger and more determined than ever to break through the iron wall. When the koan is properly presented, it never crushes this spirit but gives it greater stimulation.

It was because of this inquiring mind that the earlier Zen devotees became dissatisfied with all the intellectual explanations of things, and that they came finally to a master and knew what they wanted of him. Without this perpetual urge from within, they might have remained well contented with whatever philosophical teachings were given them in the sūtras and śastras. This urge from within was thus never to be ignored even when the koan exercise came to replace the more spontaneous rise of Zen consciousness. *San-ch'ing* or *i-ch'ing*, which is no other than this urge or this inquiring spirit, is therefore now always kept in the foreground in the study of Zen. The master's advice:

[1] That Zen was something unapproachable from its first appearance in China can easily be evinced from the legend that Bodhidharma kept up his lonely silent meditation for nine years.

I

'See where you are going to rest after death, after crema-
tion!'; or 'Exerting all your mental energies, inquire into
the final abode where the oneness of things returns'; or
'Awaken a great spirit of inquiry and see where the One
returns; do not let this spirit vacillate or falter'; or 'See
what kind of mental attitude it is, see what meaning is
yielded here, be decided to search out all that is contained
therein'; or 'Ask of your self, inquire into your self, pursue
your self, investigate within your self, and never let others
tell you what it is, nor let it be explained in words.'

When a Yogin grapples with the koan in this manner,
he is ever alive to the spirit of Zen, and so is the koan. As
the problem is a living one and not at all a dead one, satori
which follows must also be a really living experience.

Metaphysically stated, we can say that a persistent
appeal to the spirit of inquiry is based on a firm faith in
the working of Buddhatā in every individual being. It is in
fact this Buddhatā itself that leads us to inquire into the
abode of the One. The keeping up of an inquiring spirit
in Zen devotees means no less than the self-assertion of
Buddhatā. Hence the statement that 'the greater the faith
the stronger the spirit of inquiry, and the stronger the
spirit of inquiry the deeper the attainment of satori'.[1]

Faith and an inquiring spirit are not contradictory terms,
but are complementary and mutually conditioning. The
reason why the old masters were so persistent in keeping up
a great spirit of inquiry in the koan exercise becomes now
intelligible. Probably they were not conscious of the logic
that was alive behind their instruction. The presence of
Buddhatā could only be recognized by a perpetual knocking at a door, and is not this knocking an inquiring into?
The Chinese character which I have rendered 'spirit of
inquiry' literally means 'to doubt' or 'to suspect', but in the
present case 'to inquire' will be more appropriate. Thus
tai-i will mean 'great mental fixation resulting from the
utmost intensification of an inquiring spirit'.

---

[1] Quoted by Fo-chi I-an Chên in a Zen history entitled *Hui-yüan
hsü-liao*.

Hakuin writes in one of his letters, in which he treats of the relative merits of the Nembutsu[1] and the koan: 'In the study [of Zen] what is most important is the utmost intensification of an inquiring spirit. Therefore, it is said that the stronger the inquiring spirit, the greater the resulting satori, and that a sufficiently strong spirit of inquiry is sure to result in strong satori. Further, according to Fo-kuo, the greatest fault [with Zen devotees] is the lack of an inquiring spirit over the koan. When their inquiring spirit reaches its highest point of fixation there is a moment of outburst. If there are a hundred of such devotees, nay a thousand of them, I assure you, every one of them will attain the final stage. When the moment of the greatest fixation presents itself, they feel as if they were sitting in an empty space, open on all sides and extending boundlessly; they do not know whether they are living or dead; they feel so extraordinarily transparent and free from all impurities, as if they were in a great crystal basin, or shut up in an immense mass of solid ice; they are again like a man devoid of all sense; if sitting, they forget to rise, and if standing, they forget to sit.

'Not a thought, not an emotion is stirred in the mind which is now entirely and exclusively occupied with the koan itself. At this moment they are advised not to cherish any feeling of fear, to hold no idea of discrimination, but to go on resolutely ahead with their koan, when all of a sudden they experience something akin to an explosion, as if an ice basin were shattered to pieces, or as if a tower of jade had crumbled, and the event is accompanied with a feeling of immense joy such as never before has been experienced in their lives. . . . Therefore, you are instructed to inquire into the koan of "*Mu*" (*wu*) and see what sense there is in it. If your inquiring spirit is never relaxed, always intent on "*Mu*" (*wu*) and free from all ideas and emotions and imaginations, you will most decidedly attain the stage of great fixation. . . . This is all due to the presence of an inquiring spirit in you; for without that the climax will never

[1] Literally, 'thinking of the Buddha'.

be reached, and, I assure you, an inquiring spirit is the wings that bear you on to the goal.'[1]

One of the practical reasons why the mechanical method of holding the koan which is not accompanied by a spirit of inquiry is disclaimed by the masters, is that the devotee's mind becomes concentrated on mere words or sounds. This, however, may not be an altogether bad thing, as we may see later on, only that we cannot be sure of reaching, as maintained by Hakuin and others, the stage of the greatest fixation prior to the outburst of satori.

The presence of an inquiring spirit paves the way much more readily and surely to satori, because satori is what gives satisfaction to the inquiring spirit, but chiefly because the inquiring spirit awakens the faith which lies at the basis of our being. The Zen masters say, 'Where there is faith (hsin), there is doubt (i)', that is, where there is faith, there is an inquiring spirit, for doubting is believing. Let it be remarked that doubting or inquiring in Zen does not mean denying or being sceptical, it means desiring to see, to come in direct contact with the object itself, putting aside all that stands between the seer and the object. The devotee as yet has no idea as to the what of the object he wishes to see, but he believes in its existence or presence within himself. Mere description or intellectual explanation does not satisfy him, his faith is not thereby confirmed. The desire for confirmation, to see his faith solidly or absolutely established, as in the case of sense-perception, means the awakening of an inquiring spirit, and the importance of this is steadily maintained by Zen masters. If so, the mechanical repetition of the koan must be said not to be in accord with the spirit of Zen.

In a book called *Po-shan's Admonitions Regarding the Study of Zen* (*Po-shan san-ch'an ching-yü*),[2] which belongs to late Ming, the question of an inquiring spirit (*i-ch'ing*) is discussed in detail. The following is an abstract.

---

[1] From Hakuin's work known as *Orate-gama*, to which references are frequently made in this book.

[2] Wu-i Yüan-lai (1575–1630) is the author.

In striving (*kung-fu*) to master Zen, the thing needed is to cherish a strong desire to destroy a mind subject to birth and death. When this desire is awakened, the Yogin feels as if he were enveloped in a blazing fire. He wants to escape it. He cannot just be walking about, he cannot stay quietly in it, he cannot harbour any idle thoughts, he cannot expect others to help him out. Since no moment is to be lost, all he has to do is to rush out of it to the best of his strength and without being disturbed by the thought of the consequence.

Once the desire is cherished, the next step is more technical in the sense that an inquiring spirit is to be awakened and kept alive, until the final moment of solution arrives. The inquiry is concerned with the whence of birth and the whither of death, and to be constantly nourished by the desire to rise above them. This is impossible unless the spirit of inquiry is matured and breaks itself out to a state of satori.

The method of maturing consists chiefly in:

1. Not caring for worldly things.
2. Not getting attached to a state of quietude.
3. Not being disturbed by pluralities of objects.
4. Being constantly watchful over oneself, behaving like a cat who is after a mouse.
5. Concentrating one's spiritual energy on the koan.
6. Not attempting to solve it intellectually where there are no such cues in it.
7. Not trying to be merely clever about it.
8. Not taking it for a state of doing-nothing-ness.
9. Not taking a temporary state of transparency for finality.
10. Not reciting the koan as if it were the Nembutsu practice or a form of Dhāraṇī.

When these cautions are properly followed, the Yogin is sure to bring the spirit of inquiry to a state of maturity. If not, not only the spirit refuses to be awakened, but the Yogin is liable to get into wrong ways and will never be able to rise above the bondage of birth and death, that is, to realize the truth of Zen.

The wrong ways into which the Yogin may fall are:

1. Intellectualism, wherein the koan is forced to yield up its logical contents.

2. A pessimistic frame of mind whereby the Yogin shuns such environments as are unfavourable to quiet contemplation.

3. Quietism, by which he tries to suppress ideas and feelings in order to realize a state of tranquillization or perfect blankness.

4. The attempt to classify or criticize according to his own intellectualistic interpretation all the koans left by the ancient masters.

5. The understanding that there is something inside this body of the various combinations, whose intelligence shines out through the several sense-organs.

6. And which by means of the body functions to perform deeds good or bad.

7. Asceticism, in which the body is uselessly subjected to all forms of mortification.

8. The idea of merit by the accumulation of which the Yogin desires to attain Buddhahood or final deliverance.

9. Libertinism, in which there is no regulation of conduct, moral or otherwise.

10. Grandiosity and self-conceit.

These, in short, are the ways of those whose spirit of inquiry is not sincere and therefore not in accordance with the spirit of the koan exercise.

It is by means of this *i-ch'ing*, 'spirit of inquiry', that we finally attain Hakuin's *daigi* (*tai-i*), 'great fixation' or 'a state of oneness', where a mountain is not seen as such, nor a sheet of water as such, for the reason that pluralities lose their meaning and appear to the Yogin in their aspect of sameness. But that too is merely a stage in his progress towards the final realization, in which a mountain is a mountain and a sheet of water a sheet of water. When this state of great fixation is held as final, there will be no upturning, no outburst of satori, no penetration, no insight into Reality, no severing the bonds of birth and death.

PART II

1. *The Koan Exercise and the Nembutsu*

We are now in the position to see in what relation the koan exercise stands to the practice of the Nembutsu. Chinese Buddhism has developed along the two lines of Zen and Nembutsu, and to treat of their relationship means to gain knowledge concerning some of the fundamental psychological facts of the Buddhist life, and also, as I wish to maintain, of all the religious life.

Among the circumstances that led to the mechanical treatment of the koan, we may mention the prevalence of the Nembutsu in Yüan and Ming. The Nembutsu literally means, 'to think of the Buddha', and consists particularly in the recitation of the name of Amitābha Buddha (*o-mi-to-fo* in Chinese).

Historically, we can trace the origin of the Nembutsu teaching in the very early days of Buddhism in India. In China the first known group of Nembutsu devotees was the White Lotus Society led by Hui-yüan (died 416). The gradual democratization of the Buddhist faith down through the successive dynasties favoured the spread of the Nembutsu all over China and alongside of the more aristocratic Zen. Superficially considered, the Nembutsu is the very opposite of Zen, for when Zen depends on nobody outside one's self, the Nembutsu puts its reliance exclusively on the Buddha. But when the psychology of the Nembutsu is analysed there is something in the recitation of the Buddha's name as practised by the Pure Land followers, which corresponds to the holding of a koan in Zen. It was owing to this psychological common ground that their mutual approach was possible, Zen to Nembutsu and Nembutsu to Zen.

The Nembutsu was by no means mechanical in the beginning. Thinking of the Buddha came first and the invocation by name followed. But as in everything else, the content that first determined the form is later determined by the form; that is, the order is reversed. The Buddha's name may be invoked by a devotee without necessarily his thinking of the Buddha, of his excellent virtues, of his saving vows; but as he repeats the name it calls up in him all the memories and images concerning the Buddha, and without his being conscious of it, he is ever more absorbed in the contemplation of the Adored One. The invocation that was started mechanically is now turned in a direction that was not previously so designed.

The new psychology thus ushered in began to influence the adherents of the koan in late Yüan, and there were some Zen masters who took a decided stand against it. They saw the danger of the koan turning into a Nembutsu recitation, for in that case both the spirit of Zen and the reason for the koan exercise would be destroyed.

Even when the practice of the Nembutsu grew quite universal in the fifteenth century, invading even the Zen monasteries, the masters resisted the practice, advising their pupils to see *who* it is that calls upon the Buddha or recites his name. For instance, Tu-fêng Chi-shan,[1] who probably died towards the end of the fifteenth century, said: 'The main thing is to understand the ultimate meaning of life; therefore, exert yourself and spare no effort to see *who* it is that does the invoking of the name. The word *Who* is most important; concentrate yourself on this one word.'

Ch'u-shan Shao-ch'i (1404–1473) writes to one of his disciples: 'The idea of the invocation is to know that the

[1] In *The Reputed Zen Masters of the Ming Dynasty*, compiled by Chu-hung.

Buddha is no other than your own mind; but what is this mind? See into the *whence* of your thought which makes you utter the name of the Buddha; where does it originate? But you must go even farther than this and make inquiries as to the *who* of this person who wants to see into the whence of a thought. Is it mind, or Buddha, or matter? No, it is none of these, say the masters. What is it, then?'

This is the way the masters dealt with the Nembutsu in connection with the koan exercise if one wanted to master Zen. An inquiring spirit was by no means to be lost sight of. The following quotations from the Yüan and Ming Zen teachers show which way the wind was blowing in the thought world of the fourteenth and the fifteenth centuries. T'ien-ju Wei-tsê, who flourished early in the fourteenth century, was a great figure during the Yüan dynasty, and there is no doubt that the Nembutsu movement was going on quite strongly then and encroaching upon the realm of Zen. Wei-tsê could not ignore it and wished to define clearly where Zen differed from Nembutsu and how far the one agreed with the other. In the second volume of his *Sayings* (*yü-lu*) it is written:

'There are some these days among the laity as well as in the Brotherhood who desire by means of the Nembutsu to be born in the Land of Purity and wonder if the Nembutsu is not to be distinguished from Zen. In my view, they fail to recognize that Zen and Nembutsu are not the same and yet are the same; for the object of Zen is to understand what life means, and the object of the Nembutsu is also that. Zen directly points to the mind in every one of us, declaring that to see into the nature of every being means attaining Buddhahood; whereas the Nembutsu aims at reaching the Land of Purity which is no other than one's own mind, and seeing into the original nature of every being which is Amitābha himself.

'If this is so, how can one differentiate Nembutsu from Zen? We read in a sūtra that it is like entering into a great city which is provided with gates on its four sides; people coming from different quarters will find their own entrance as there is more than one gate. But, once in, they are in the same city. Zen and Nembutsu each appeals to a special type of character; that is all.

'In the Nembutsu you can distinguish between that which is effective and that which is not. Why? If the devotee's invocation does not go farther than his lips while his mind is not at all thinking of the Buddha, this kind of invocation is not effective. If on the other hand his lips and his mind are conjointly working towards the Buddha as his name is recited, so that his mind always works in union with the Buddha, his Nembutsu will surely bring its result. Suppose here is a man carrying a rosary in his hand and reciting the Buddha's name with his lips; but if in the meantime his thoughts are all in confusion, running wild in every direction, he is the one whose invocation is on his lips only and not in his mind. He is uselessly fatiguing himself, his labour comes to naught. It is far better to be thinking of the Buddha in the mind even though the lips are not moving, for such is the real follower of the Nembutsu.

'Do we not read in a sūtra that all the Tathāgatās in the ten quarters are lovingly thinking of all beings just as a mother does of her children; for beings that are drowning in the ocean of birth and death are like children who are wandering in strange foreign countries. The Buddha like a loving mother thinks of them, and though he may not be talking about his compassionate feeling, his heart never ceases thinking of his lost children. If the children thought of their mother in the same way, will not they, mother and children, some day come face to face?

'Therefore, the sūtra says that if the hearts of all beings long for the Buddha and think of him they will surely see him either in the present or in the future. The present means this life, the future means the life to come. If this is so, he who intensely longs for the Buddha and thinks of him, will most assuredly come into his presence. What then is the difference between coming into the presence of the Buddha and attaining satori by the study of Zen?

'Says the Master Huan-chu: The study of Zen aims at

elucidating the meaning of birth and death, whereas the Nembutsu proposes to get settled with the question of death and birth; choose either one of the pathways, for there is no disputation to be aroused about them. Quite true, there is no disputation between the two, but do not allow yourself to keep both with you. Let the Zen devotee keep himself exclusively to Zen, and let the one who recites the Nembutsu keep exclusively to the Nembutsu. If the mind is divided between the two, neither will be attained. There is a comparision drawn by an old master between such a divided mind and a man who tries to be in two boats simultaneously and is in neither. So far, there is no harm, perhaps, but a worse case may come to him at any moment, for he may fall between the two boats if he does not look out for himself.

'As for myself, I do not know much, but this I can tell, that in the Nembutsu just these four syllables are held up: *O-mi-to-fo* (*a-mi-da-butsu* in Japanese), which indicates no way, at least to Zen beginners, as to how to proceed with it. They are naturally at a loss, and fail to know what to do with the subject. But in the study of the koan you are told that you are each in possession of "the original face" which is the same as it is in all the Buddhas, only that in us it is not recognized. Try and see into it all by yourself without depending on anyone else. In this it may be said that you have a kind of clue whereby to go on with your Zen.'

One of the first Zen masters to introduce the idea of Nembutsu into Zen was Yang-ming Yen-shou.[1] He laid great importance on Zen Yogins devoting themselves to the practice of the Nembutsu to this extent, that he declared that those who follow Zen without Nembutsu may fail nine out of ten in their attainment of the final goal, whereas those who practise Nembutsu will all without exception come to realization; but the best are those who practise Zen and Nembutsu, for they will be like a tiger provided with horns. What Yang-ming exactly means by this statement is not easy to comprehend, for he does not tell us as to its

[1] Died 975.

practical side; that is, how to practise both Zen and Nembutsu at the same time. Did he mean to practise the Nembutsu after the attainment of Zen, or *vice versa*? Until this practical question is definitely settled, we may not venture either to refute or to defend Yang-ming.

This much we can say, that the Nembutsu had been making steady progress even among followers of Zen as early as the tenth century, and Yang-ming, as one of the greatest syncretists China ever produced, attempted to include into his system of Zen philosophy every school of Buddhism, and the Nembutsu naturally came to be fused into it. Besides, there was another strong reason why Zen had to listen to the appeal of the Nembutsu, which was this. Zen being too philosophical (though not in the ordinary sense of the term) exposed itself to an utter disregard of the emotional side of life. Zen indulges itself in excessive satori, so to speak, and as the result it frequently dries up its tears which must be shed over ignorance, over the miseries of life, over the world filled with iniquity. Thus Zen holds out no hope for a land of bliss and purity which is so vividly felt by the followers of Nembutsu. Did Yang-ming mean this when he said that Zen must be accompanied by the Nembutsu? The following remarks made by K'ung-ku Ching-lung, who flourished early in the fifteenth century, seem at least partly to point this interpretation. He says:

'Those who practise Zen are so exclusively devoted to Zen, thinking that they are thus exerting themselves to the attainment of quietude and nothing else: as to invoking the name of the Buddha in order to be born in the Land of Purity and worshipping him and reciting the sūtras in the morning and evening, they practise nothing of the sort. Such devotees may be called those who have Zen but have no Nembutsu. Yet really those followers of Zen are not of the right kind; they are mere sticklers of the koan exercise, they are quite like a stick or stone or brick. When they are attacked by this form of mental disease, they cannot be saved, except perhaps only one out of ten.

'Zen is a living spirit; it is like a gourd floating on water, when you touch it it dances most lively. Therefore, it is said that regard should be paid to the living spirit of the masters and not to their dead words. But there are others who practising Zen do not slight the teaching of the Nembutsu school and will regularly attend the morning and evening services. Indeed, the truth of Zen is met with anywhere you go if you only look for it. Hsüeh-fêng laboured hard as cook wherever he went, and Yang-chi busied himself as overseer of the monastery; they never made light of their daily life while innerly they devoted themselves to Zen. Yang-ming mastered the Zen of his teacher, Tê-shao, and yet was well disposed to propagate the doctrine of the Pure Land school. Is he not one who innerly was round and outwardly square? Innerly, he was all that could be desired of a Bodhisattva, and outwardly, acted as if he were one who belonged to the Śrāvakas. He is one who has both Zen and Nembutsu.'[1]

There is something lame in this interpretation, but the fact is not to be denied that the Nembutsu was rapidly undermining the strongholds of Zen in those days, and we will presently see that in the psychology of the Nembutsu there is a factor that can readily ally itself with the koan exercise in its mechanical phase. For in spite of this attitude of K'ung-ku towards the Nembutsu as a kind of Śrāvaka practice, he proceeds to uphold it as of the same efficiency as the koan exercise in the realization of the true Buddhist life.

In K'ung-ku's letter to another of his disciples, which was evidently written in answer to an inquiry concerning the practice of Nembutsu, the author advises him just to say the Nembutsu not necessarily with a philosophical attitude of mind; that is, with no inquiring spirit. The main point in the Nembutsu is to have a believing heart and quietly say it without troubling oneself about things of this world. Ku says:

'The doctrine of the Nembutsu is the shortest road to the realization of the Buddhist life. Be convinced of the

[1] From a letter to one of his disciples as quoted in Chu-hung's *Ming Masters*.

unrealness of this bodily existence, for to get attached to the vanities of this worldly life is the cause of transmigration. What is most desirable is the Land of Purity and what is most dependable is the Nembutsu. No matter how you are thinking of the Buddha, intensely or leisurely, no matter how you are invoking his name, whether loudly or softly, do not allow yourself to be constrained by any rule, but keep your mind unruffled, restful, and in silent contemplation. When it attains a state of unity undisturbed by environment, some day an accident will unexpectedly cause in you a sort of mental revolution, and thereby you will realize that the Pure Land of Serene Light is no less than this earth itself, and Amitābha Buddha is your own mind. But you must be careful not to let your mind expectantly wait for such a momentous event, for this will prove a hindrance to the realization itself.

'The Buddha-nature is a spontaneous generation in the sense that it is not a product of intellection, nor of imagination. When I say this, however, you may take it for a state of unconsciousness, which is another great error to be avoided. The only thing that is essential in this connection is to have a believing heart and not to allow any unnecessary and disturbing thoughts to become mixed in it. As you go on thus in the practice of Nembutsu while you may have no chance of attaining satori in this life, you will after death surely be reborn in the Pure Land, where by going up various grades you will finally arrive at the position which never turns back.

'The master Yu-t'an makes people hold this : "Who is it that practises the Nembutsu? What is it that is my own nature, which is, Amitābha?" This may be called the Nembutsu said in a strained state of mind or the Nembutsu accompanied with an inquiring spirit. It is not necessary for you to follow this method ; just say your Nembutsu in an ordinary frame of mind.'

K'ung-ku's advice that the Nembutsu is not necessarily to be backed by an intensification of an inquiring spirit opens the way to the mechanical method of invocation.

This is what made Hakuin and his school rise furiously against some of the Chinese Zen masters of the fourteenth century and after.

Chu-hung, the author of the *Ming Masters*, the *Frontier Gate of Zen*, and many other works, who was also bitterly attacked by Hakuin, comments on K'ung-ku Ching-lung: 'Most Zen teachers tell people to see who he is that invokes the Buddha's name, but Ching-lung states that this is not absolutely necessary. As medicine is to be prescribed according to disease, so is the truth to be taught according to capacity. Each of these two is justifiable and there is no option to be made between them.'[1]

This method of invocation endorsed by such masters as Ching-lung and Chu-hung is based on psychological facts, and the subject may better be approached now from the viewpoint of the Nembutsu and not from that of Zen. Let us then see what is really meant by the Nembutsu.

2. *Nembutsu* (*nien-fo*) *and Shōmyō* (*ch'êng-ming*)

Nembutsu or *buddhānusmṛiti* literally means 'to think of the Buddha', or 'to meditate on the Buddha', and is counted as one of the six subjects of meditation in the *Mahāvyutpatti*. The six are as follows: 1. *Buddhānusmṛiti*; 2. *Dharma*; 3. *Samgha* (Brotherhood); 4. *Śīla* (morality); 5. *Tyāga* (giving up); and 6. *Devatā* (gods). It is also one of the five subjects of mental discipline known as *Wu t'ing hsin*; that is, objects by thinking of which the mind is kept away from erroneous views. The five are: 1. Impurity of the body, the thought of which reacts against greed and lust; 2. Compassion, as against anger; 3. Causation, as against infatuation or folly; 4. The six elements, as against the notion of an ego-substance; and 5. Breathing exercise, as against mental perturbation. Though I am unable to find out exactly how it came to pass, the fourth subject (that is, the six elements: earth, water, fire, air, the void, and consciousness) is

[1] *Biographies of the Famous Ming Masters.*

replaced by 'meditation on the Buddha' (*nembutsu*) in Chih-chê's commentary on the *Saddharmapuṇḍarīka*. According to a work belonging to the T'ien-tai school of Chih-chê, this meditation is considered to counteract mental heaviness, evil thoughts, and physical calamities.

It is a very natural thing for the Buddhists to meditate on their teacher, whose great personality impressed them in some way more than did his teaching. When they were not feeling energetic in their search after the truth, or when their minds were disturbed by all kinds of worldly temptation, the best way to strengthen their moral courage was, no doubt, to think of their teacher. In the beginning the Nembutsu was a purely moral practice, but as the mysterious power of a name came to claim a stronger hold on the religious imagination of the Indian Buddhists, the thinking of the Buddha as a person endowed with great virtues ceased and gave way to the uttering of his name. As a philosopher says, *Nec nomen Deo quaeras ; Deus nomen est*. Name is as good as substance; in some cases it works far more efficaciously than that for which it stands, for when we know the name, we can put a god into service. This has been so from the earliest days of every religious history all the world over. When Amitābha Buddha obtained his enlightenment he wished to have his name (*nāmadheya*) resound throughout the great chiliocosms, so that he might save any being that heard his name.[1]

But the sūtra[2] makes no reference yet to the uttering of his name only. The phrases used are: *daśabhiś cittot-pādaparivartaiḥ*,[3] which forms the nineteenth vow of the

[1] See the *Sukhāvatīvyūha Sūtra*.

[2] This is one of the three principal sutras belonging to the Pure Land school. The three are: 1. *Sukhāvatīvyūha*, which treats of the Land of Bliss inhabited by Amitābha Buddha, and of the forty-eight (forty-three in the Sanskrit text) vows of the same Amitābha; 2. *Sūtra of the Meditations on Buddha Amitāyus*, in which Queen Vaidehī is instructed by Śākyamuni to practise sixteen forms of meditation regarding the Land of Bliss and its Lord; and 3. *The Sūtra of Amitābha*, which is generally known as the *Smaller Sukhāvatīvyūha*, as it also describes the Land of Bliss. Amitāyus (Eternal Life) and Amitābha (Infinite Light) refer to one and the same Buddha.

[3] Max Muller, p. 15, l. 4.

Sanskrit text, meaning 'Ten times repeating the thought [of the Pure Land]'; *prasannacittā mām anusmareyuh*,[1] which is the eighteenth vow of the Sanskrit text, meaning 'Remembered me with pure thoughts'; or *antaśa ekacittotpādam api adhyāśayena prasādasahagatena cittam utpādayanti*,[2] '[All beings] raise their thought, even for once only, raise their thought, with devotion and serenity.' *Cittotpāda* or *anusmṛiti*, 'thinking of [the Buddha]' is not the same as 'uttering the name'.

The *Pratyutpanna-samādhi-Sūtra* which was translated into Chinese as early as the second century by Lokaraksha, in which mention is also made of Amitābha Buddha in the West, and which is consequently regarded as one of the authoritative sources of the Pure Land school, refers to the name of the Buddha, saying 'The Bodhisattva, who hearing the name of the Buddha Amitābha wishes to see him, may see him by constantly thinking of the region where he is.' The term used here is 'thinking' (*nien* in Chinese) and not 'uttering'. Whenever the Buddha becomes an object of meditation, no matter to what school the devotee may belong, Hīnayāna or Mahāyāna, Zen or Shin, he has been thought of as a personality, not only physically, but as spiritually inspiring.

In the *Sūtra of the Meditation on the Buddha of Eternal Life*, however, the devotees are taught to say 'Adoration to Buddha Amitābha'; for when they utter this Buddha-name they will be liberated from sins committed in their lives for fifty billions of kalpas. Again, if a dying man cannot think of the Buddha owing to intense pain, he is told just to utter the name of the Buddha of Eternal Life (*Amitāyus*). In the *Smaller Sukhāvatīvyūha*, or *Sūtra of Amitāyus*, the author advises people to hold in mind (*manasikara*) the name of the blessed Amitāyus the Tathāgatā, which will make them depart with a tranquil mind from this life, when the time comes.

In accordance with these instructions in the sūtras,

[1] Max Muller, p. 14, l. 15.
[2] Max Muller, p. 47, ll. 2, 3.

K

Nāgārjuna writes in his *Commentary on the Daśabhūmika* (Chapter V, 'On Easy Practice') that if one wishes quickly to reach the stage of no-turning-back, he should hold the Buddha's name in mind full of reverent thought. There may be some difference, as far as words go, between 'holding in mind' and 'uttering' or 'invoking', but, practically, holding the Buddha's name in mind is to utter it with the lips, silently or audibly. The shifting of the centre of devotional attention from thinking to utterance, from remembrance to invocation, is a natural process.

Tao-ch'o[1] quotes a sūtra in his *Book of Peace and Happiness*,[2] which is one of the principal sources of the Pure Land doctrine. All the Buddhas save beings in four ways: 1. By oral teachings such as are recorded in the twelve divisions of Buddhist literature; 2. By their physical features of supernatural beauty; 3. By their wonderful powers and virtues and transformations; and 4. By their names, which, when uttered by beings, will remove obstacles and assure their rebirth in the presence of the Buddha.

To this Tao-ch'o adds: 'To my mind the present age belongs to the fourth five-hundred-years after the Buddha, and what we have to do now is to repent our sins, to cultivate virtues, and to utter the Buddha's name. Is it not said that even once thinking of Amitābha Buddha and uttering his name cleanses us from all our sins committed while transmigrating for eighty billion kalpas? If even one thought achieves this, how much more if one constantly thinks of the Buddha and repents one's [sinful deeds]!' All the Nembutsu followers who came after him have eagerly accepted his teaching, and *nembutsu* (*nien-fo*), 'thinking of the Buddha', has become identified with *shōmyō* (*ch'êng-ming*), 'uttering the name'.

In fact, uttering the name contains more and functions more effectively than thinking of the various excellent spiritual virtues and physical qualities with which the Buddha is endowed. The name represents all that can be

---

[1] 562–645, one of the foremost devotees of the Pure Land teaching.
[2] *An-lê-chi.*

predicated of the Buddha. The thinking of him means holding up his image in mind, and all kinds of hallucinations are apt to appear before the eye. In the case of the name, the mental operations tend more towards intellection, and a different psychology obtains here.

Here we can distinguish two ways in which the Buddha-name can be invoked; that is, when the name is announced, there are two attitudes on the part of the devotee towards the object of his adoration. In one case, the invocation takes place with the idea that *nomen est numen*, or as a sort of magical formula. The name itself is regarded as having some mysterious power to work wonders. For instance, we read in the *Saddharmapuṇḍarīka*, Chapter XXIV, where the worship of Avalokiteśvara is upheld:

'[Goblins and giants] would, by virtue of the name of Bodhisattva-Mahāsattva Avalokiteśvara being pronounced, lose the faculty of sight in their designs.' Or, 'Be not afraid, invoke all of you with one voice the Bodhisattva-Mahāsattva Avalokiteśvara, the giver of safety, then you shall be delivered from this danger by which you are threatened at the hands of robbers and enemies.'

In these cases the name of Avalokiteśvara has undoubtedly a magical power not only over one's enemies, but also over impure passions, hatred, infatuation, etc. It further enables the devotee to get whatever happiness he desires. The gāthās in this chapter describe all the virtues issuing from him, and what the devotee has to do is just to think of him; that is, to utter his name. It was quite natural in the light here shed by the name of Avalokiteśvara that scholars of Shin Buddhism had once a heated discussion regarding the wonderful saving power of Amitābha, asking whether it comes from his name or from his vows.

The other attitude which may be assumed by the devotee towards the invocation, or Nembutsu, is especially represented by T'ien-ju Wei-tsê, a Zen master of the Yüan dynasty of the fourteenth century. He states in his *Some Questions Regarding the Pure Land Answered*:

'The Nembutsu consists in intensely thinking of the

thirty-two marks of excellence possessed by the Buddha, by holding them in mind in a state of concentration, when one will see the Buddha all the time whether his eyes are closed or open. This seeing the Buddha while still in this life may also take place when the Buddha is invoked by name, which is held fast in the mind. This way of coming into the presence of the Buddha by invoking him by name is better than the Nembutsu. When you practise this invocation, the mind must be kept under full control so that it will not wander about; let your thought dwell without interruption on the name of the Buddha, audibly repeat *O-mi-to-fo*[1] (or *nembutsu*). Each sound must be distinctly presented to the mind. Do not mind how many times the name is repeated, for the main thing is to have thought and will, mind and lips, all in perfect union.'

In the first case the name itself is regarded as having a wonderful power, especially over human affairs; it is a magic formula. When Amitābha wished to have his name resound all over the universe, did he want it to be a sort of talisman, or did he want it to be a moral force; that is, symbolic of something that is desirable in human life, so that whenever his name was heard his virtues and merits would be remembered, and would serve to incite the hearers to follow his example? Most likely the latter was in his mind. When the name is uttered, all that it stands for is awakened in the mind of the utterer; not only that, but finally his own mind will thereby open up its deepest resources and reveal its inmost truth which is no other than the reality of the name; that is, Amitābha himself.

In the second case, the name is pronounced not necessarily as indicative of things that are therein suggested, but in order to work out a certain psychological process thus set up. The name of the Buddha may now even be mechanically repeated without reference to the bearer of the name himself as an objective reality. This is what has actually taken place later in the history of the koan exercise. The following incident which took place in the mind of an old

[1] *A-mi-da-butsu.*

miser under the instruction of Hakuin, founder of the modern Japanese Rinzai School of Zen Buddhism, will supply us with a good illustration of what I mean by the psychological process induced by the recitation of the Buddha-name.

One of the numerous lay-disciples of Hakuin was worried over his old miserly father whose mind so bent on making money was not at all disposed towards Buddhism. He wanted Hakuin to suggest some method to turn his father's thought away from avarice. Hakuin suggested this proposal: Let the miserly old gentleman say the Nembutsu whenever he thinks of it, and have a penny paid for each recital. If he said the Nembutsu for one hundred times a day, he would have one hundred pennies for it.

The old man thought that it was the easiest way in the world to earn his pocket money. He came each day to Hakuin to be paid for his Nembutsu as he was perfectly regular in his account, so much for so many repetitions. He was enchanted with his earnings. But after a while he ceased to come to Hakuin for his daily payment. Hakuin sent for the son to learn what was the matter with the father. It was found that the father was now so engrossed in saying the Nembutsu that he forgot to make a record of it. This was what Hakuin was all the time expecting of him. He told the devoted son to leave his father alone for some time and see what would become of him now. The advice was followed, and in a week the father himself came up to Hakuin with beaming eyes, which told at once what a blissful spiritual experience he had gone through. There was no doubt that he had a kind of satori.

The mechanical repetition of the Nembutsu, that is, the rhythmic though monotonous utterance of the Buddha name, 'na-mu-a-mi-da-bu', 'na-mu-a-mi-da-bu' . . . over again and again, tens of thousands of times, creates a state of consciousness which tends to keep down all the ordinary functions of the mind. This state is very much akin perhaps to that of hypnotic trance, but fundamentally different from the latter in that what grows out of the Nembutsu consciousness is a most significant insight into the nature of Reality and has a most enduring and beneficial effect on the spiritual life of the devotee. In a hypnotic trance there is nothing of the sort, for it is a diseased state of mind bearing no fruit of a permanent value.

As regards the difference between the koan exercise and the Nembutsu, as was already repeatedly pointed out, in the one it consists in the absence of the intellectual element, and in the other in the presence of an inquiring spirit.

3. *The Value of Shōmyō* ('*Uttering the Name*') *in the Jōdo school*

After the decease of the Buddha the earnest desire of his followers was to see him again. They could not persuade themselves to think that such a great personality as the Buddha had completely passed away from among them. The impression he had left in their minds was too deep to be wiped off so soon and so easily. This is generally the case with any great soul. We are loath to consider his physical death the ending of all that constituted him, all that be- longed to him; we want to believe that he is still alive among us, not in his former worldly fashion but in some way, perhaps in the way we like to designate spiritual. Thinking so, we are sure to see him somewhere and sometime.

This was true with the Christ as with the Buddha. But the Buddha had been living among a people who were trained in all kinds of concentration called Samādhi, and who were also perfect masters of practical psychology. The result was the production of such sūtras as the *Meditation Sūtra* (*Kwangyo*) or the *Pratyutpannasamādhi Sūtra* (*Han-jusammai*), in which directions are given in detail for having a personal interview with the Buddha or the Buddhas. First, there must be an intense thinking of the past master, an earnest longing to see him once more, and then, the spiritual exercise in which the thinking and longing is to be visualized —this is the natural order of things.

This visualization seems to have taken two courses as time went on: the one was nominalistic[1] and the other idealistic. It is of significance that these two tendencies are traceable in one and the same sūtra which is entitled *Sapta-śatikā-prajñā-pāramitā Sūtra*,[2] which was translated into Chinese by Man-t'o-lo-hsein of Fu-nan-kuo in A.D. 503, of the Liang dynasty. The sūtra belongs to the Prajñāpāramitā class of Mahāyāna literature and is considered to be one of the earliest Mahāyāna texts. It contains the essence of Prajñāpāramitā philosophy, but what strikes us as strange is that the two tendencies of thought, nominalistic and idealistic, apparently contradicting each other, are presented here side by side. I suspect the later incorporation of the passages referring to the nominalistic current of thought which is made so much of by the expositors of the Pure Land teaching. However this may be, the visualizing process of meditation is generally superseded in this sūtra by the idealization of Buddhahood, which is typical of all the Prajñā texts.

In the opening passage of this sūtra, Mañjuśrī expresses his desire to interview the Buddha in his true aspect, thus:

'I desire to see the Buddha as he is in order to benefit all beings. I see the Buddha in the aspect of suchness (*tathatā*), of no-other-ness, of immovability, of doing-nothing-ness; I see the Buddha as free from birth and death, from form and no-form, from spatial and temporal relations, from duality and non-duality, from defilement and purity. Thus seen, he is in his true aspect and all beings are thereby benefited.

[1] It is not quite proper to use a scholastic term in this connection, but my idea is to distinguish here the aspect of the Nembutsu exercise in which the significance of the name is held up more emphatically against all other considerations. By 'nominalism', therefore, I wish to indicate roughly the principle operating in the emphatical upholding of the name as efficacious to mature the Samādhi of Oneness, or in being born in the Pure Land of Amitābha. 'Idealism' or 'conceptualism' will then mean the attitude of Prajñāpāramitā philosophers who endeavour to describe the ultimate nature of Reality by means of highly abstract, conceptualistic terms which are generally negativistic.

[2] There are three Chinese translations of this sūtra, the first of which appeared in A.D. 503 and the last in A.D. 693. It is generally known as a sūtra on Prajñāpāramitā expounded by Mañjuśrī. The Buddhist Tripitaka, Taisho Edition, Nos. 232, 233, and 220 (7).

'By seeing the Buddha in this manner [the Bodhisattva] is freed from both attachment and non-attachment, both accumulation and dissipation. . . .

'While thus seeing the Buddha for the sake of all beings, his [Bodhisattva's] mind is not attached to the form of all beings. While teaching all beings so as to make them turn towards Nirvāṇa, he is not attached to the form of Nirvāṇa. While arranging varieties of things in order for the sake of all beings, the mind does not recognize them [as having individual realities].'

In another version by Saṁghapāla, which appeared a few years later than Man-t'o-lo's, we have this:

'Buddha asked: Do you really wish to see the Buddha?

'Mañjuśrī said: The Dharmakāya of the Buddha is not really to be seen. That I come to see the Buddha here is for the sake of all things. As to the Dharmakāya of the Buddha, it is beyond thinkability, it has no form, no shape, it is neither coming nor departing, neither existent nor non-existent, neither visible nor invisible, it is such as it is, it is reality-limit. This light [that emanates from the Buddha giving a supernatural power to those who can perceive it] is Prajñāpāramitā, and Prajñāpāramitā is the Tathāgata, and the Tathāgata is all beings; and it is in this way that I practise Prajñāpāramitā.'

In Man-t'o-lo's translation, this Prajñāpāramitā is defined to be 'limitless, boundless, nameless, formless, beyond speculation, with nothing to depend on, with no anchorage, neither offensive nor blessed, neither darkening nor illuminating, neither divisible nor countable. . . . And when this is experienced, one is said to have attained enlightenment.'

The thought expressed here is in perfect agreement with what generally characterizes the philosophy of the *Prajñāpāramitā Sūtras*. The Buddha here is described in highly abstract terms by a series of negations. While the idea Buddha thus does not appear to go beyond verbalism (*adhivacana*), he is after all more than a mere name (*nāmadheya*). Any amount of negations, it is true, fails to make one grasp the suchness of Buddhahood, but this does not of course mean that the Buddha, or what is the same thing, Prajñāpāramitā or supreme enlightenment, can be realized by merely repeating his name. If this is possible, the uttering of the Buddha-name must be considered in some other light; that is, not in the sense of abstract negation, but in the psychological process started by the repetition itself. It is interesting to see this shifting of thought from conceptualism to psychological realism. Let us see what Mañjuśrī has further to say about supreme enlightenment to be attained by means of the Buddha-name (nāmadheya).

In the second half of the Saptaśatikā-Prajñāpāramitā (Man-t'o-lo version) a Samādhi known as i-hsing[1] is mentioned, whereby the Yogin realizes supreme enlightenment and also comes into the presence of the Buddhas of the past, present, and future. The passage in the Man-t'o-lo runs as follows:

'Again, there is the Samādhi i-hsing; when this Samādhi is practised by sons and daughters of good family, supreme enlightenment will speedily be realized by them.

Mañjuśrī asked, 'Blessed One, what is this i-hsing Samādhi?'

The Blessed One said: 'The Dharmadhātu is characterized with oneness, and as the Samādhi is conditioned by [this oneness of] the Dharmadhātu it is called the Samādhi

---

[1] 'Samādhi of One Deed (?)', in Man-t'o-lo's version, is the 'Samādhi of One Form Array' (ekanimitta (?) vyūhasamādhi) in Hsüan-tsang's translation. In the Sanskrit text now extant this Samādhi is called ekavyūhasamādhi. Vyūha is generally rendered as chuang-yen in Chinese, meaning 'embellishment', 'array', or 'arrangement in order'. The sense is, however, not to arrange things merely for the sake of decoration; it is to fill the abstract barrenness of Reality with multiplicities, and it may be regarded sometimes as synonymous with 'individualization', or 'particular objects'. Ekavyūha, therefore, may mean 'one particular object' and ekavyūha-samādhi 'a samādhi with one object in view'. It is difficult to take hsing to be equivalent to vyūha, for hsing is usually caryā.

The passage containing the account of the i-hsing samādhi is missing in Saṁghapāla's translation, which fact suggests its later addition. Probably the earlier text of the Saptaśatikā-Prajñāpāramitā Sūtra thoroughly retained the characteristic features of Prajñā-pāramitā philosophy with no admixture of the visualizing meditation and also of the nominalistic trend of thought.

of Oneness (*i-hsing*). If sons and daughters of good family wish to enter upon this Samādhi of Oneness they must listen to the discourse on Prajñāpāramitā and practise it accordingly; for then they can enter upon the Samādhi of Oneness whereby they will realize the Dharmadhātu in its aspect of not-going-back, of not-being-destroyed, of un-thinkability, of non-obstruction, of no-form.

'If sons and daughters of good family wish to enter upon the Samādhi of Oneness, let them sit in a solitary place, abandon all thoughts that are disturbing, not become attached to forms and features, have the mind fixed on one Buddha, and devote themselves exclusively to reciting (*ch'êng*) his name (*ming*, or *nāmadheya*), sitting in the proper style in the direction where the Buddha is, and facing him squarely. When their thoughts are continuously fixed on one Buddha, they will be able to see in these thoughts all the Buddhas of the past, present, and future. . . .'[1]

In Man-t'o-lo's text there is a strange mixture of Prajñā-pāramitā philosophy proper with the visualization of the Buddha by means of his name, which is recited with single-ness of thought. Hsüan-tsang's text refers to reflecting on the personality of personal features of the Buddha in con-nection with holding his name, which to a certain extent contradicts the idea of the first text. For the first one em-phasizes the uttering of the name with no allusion what-ever to visualizing the personal marks of Buddhahood, and yet it promises the Yogins their seeing not only one Buddha whose name they recite but all the Buddhas of the past, present, and future. And this is indeed the point upon which

---

[1] In the Hsüan-tsang version no reference is made to the recitation (*ch'êng*), thus: 'If sons and daughters of good family wish to enter upon this Samādhi, let them retire to a solitary place away from confusions, and sit cross-legged without thinking of forms of any kind; let them, in order to benefit all sentient beings, single-mindedly and collectively take hold of the [Buddha's] name and reflect well on his personality, while turning in the direction where the Buddha is and facing him in the proper attitude. To have their thoughts continually fixed on this one Buddha is thereby to see all the Buddhas of the past, present, and future.'

In the Sanskrit *Saptaśatikā*, we have simply '*tasya nāmadheyaṁ grahi-tavyan*'.

the Pure Land followers lay great emphasis in their teaching; that is, the sutra's preference given to verbal or nominalistic recitation rather than reflection or visualization.

In the *Pratyutpanna-samādhi Sūtra*[1] also, the visualizing meditation singularly blends with the nominalistic trends of thought. The subject of discourse here as given to the Bodhisattva Bhadrapāla is how to realize a Samādhi known as Pratyutpanna, in which all the Buddhas of the ten quarters come and stand before the Yogin ready to answer all the questions he may ask them. The Yogin's qualifications are:

1. He must have great faith in the Buddha; 2. He must exert himself to the farthest extent of his spiritual energy; 3. He must be provided with a thorough understanding of the Dharma; and 4. He must always be associated with good friends and teachers. When these conditions are fulfilled, the Samādhi is matured, and then, first, because of the sustaining power of the Buddha which is added to the Yogin; secondly, because of the virtue of the Samādhi itself; and, thirdly, because of the virtue inherent in the accumulated stock of merit, all the Buddhas appear before the Yogin in such a manner as images are reflected in a mirror.

In the beginning the Yogin hears of the name of the Buddha Amitābha and his Land of Purity. By means of this name, he visualizes all the excellent and extraordinary features belonging to the Buddha, such as his thirty-two major marks of manhood and eighty minor ones. The Yogin will also visualize all the resplendent glories of the Buddha while reflecting (*nien*) on his name with singleness of thought.

When this exercise attains its fullness, the Yogin's mind is purged of all its impurities. As it grows pure, the Buddha is

---

[1] This is also known as the *Bhadrapāla Bodhisattva Sūtra* because this is the name of the interlocutor in the sūtra. There are four extant Chinese translations of it. The first one was done by Lou-chia-ch'ien as early as A.D. 179. It is one of the authoritative sources of the Pure Land teaching. See also pp. 171 *f.*

reflected in it, and the mind and the Buddha are finally identified, as if the mind is looking at itself or the Buddha at himself, and yet the Yogin is not conscious of this fact of self-identification. To be thus unconscious is Nirvāṇa. When there is the slightest stirring of a thought the identification scale is tipped, and there starts a world of infatuations.

Strictly speaking, it is doubtful whether the sūtra makes so much of the name and its recitation as is maintained by the followers of the Pure Land. As far as we can see, the visualization plays as much importance as thinking of the name. It is true that without a name our minds are unable to take hold of anything; even when there is really something objectively in existence, so long as it remains unnamed it has no reality for us. When a thing gets its name, its relations with other things are defined and its value fully appreciated. Amitābha is non-existent when we cannot invoke him by a name; naming is creating, so to speak. But, on the other hand, mere naming does not prove to be so efficient, is not so effect-producing, as when there is back of it a corresponding reality. Mere uttering the name 'water' does not quench the thirst; when it is visualized and there is a mental picture of a spring it produces a more physiologically realistic effect; but it is only when there is real fresh water before us which is quaffed that the thirst actually eases.

By means of sheer will and imagination, the mental picture can attain the highest degree of intensification, but there is naturally a limit to human powers. When this limit is reached, a leap into the abyss is possible only by the sustaining power which is now added to the Yogin by the Buddhas of the ten quarters. Thus the name, reflection or visualization and actualization are the natural order of things playing the most important role in the system of the Pure Land teaching.

It was owing to Shan-tao's[1] pietistic synthesis that the visualizing meditation, the nominalistic attitude, and the

[1] Died A.D. 681.

rebirth in the Pure Land were made to form a system, which was to be put into active service by means of the Nembutsu; that is, by constantly and singlemindedly pronouncing the name of Amitābha Buddha. After him, visualization gradually ceased to be upheld and nominalism came to reign over the entire school of the Pure Land. In China the koan exercise had about this time probably been gaining influence along with the prevalence of nominalism, but in Japan the establishment of the Pure Land school as an independent sect greatly helped the growth of the Nembutsu; that is, the vocal Nembutsu.

The transition of emphasis from idealism to nominalism, from the singleminded thinking to the vocal recitation, may be traced in the following passage from the *An-lê-chi* of Tao-ch'o, who answers the question how the Nembutsu is to be practised:

'It is like a man travelling through the wilderness who happens to be attacked by a highwayman. The latter savagely threatens the traveller at the point of the sword and if his order is not obeyed, is ready to murder him. The traveller fleeing away from the impending peril observes a stream before him. Before reaching it, he reflects: "When I come to the river, should I cross it with my dress on or not? As to undressing myself there may not be time enough for it. But even when I jump into it with all my things on, my head and neck may not be safe enough from the attack." At this critical moment he has indeed no other thought than devising the way to get to the other side of the river. His mind is exclusively devoted to it. It is the same with the devotee of the Nembutsu. When he thinks of the Buddha Amitābha, his mind should be exclusively occupied with the thought, so that it has no room left for anything else.

'Whether he thinks (*nien*) of the Dharmakāya of the Buddha, or of his supernatural powers, or of his Prajñā, or of the light issuing from his hair-tuft, or of his physical features, or of his Original Vow, let the devotee uninterruptedly pronounce (*ch'êng*) the name of the Buddha with singleness of thought so that no room is left in his mind for anything else, and he is sure to be reborn in the presence of the Buddha.'

At such a critical moment as described here it is doubted whether the devotee has enough room left in his mind to do any sort of reflection. All that he can do will be pronouncing the name of the Buddha, for he cannot have any psychological time which is to be devoted to thinking of the Buddha's virtues or powers or features. In this case his Nembutsu (*nien-fo*, literally, 'thinking of the Buddha') cannot be more than a *shōmyō* (*ch'êng-ming*, literally, 'pronouncing or uttering the name'). For in the pronouncing of the name of the Buddha, that is, in reciting the Nembutsu, his whole being is absorbed; this is all he can do consciously, there can be no other thoughts in his field of consciousness.

Shan-tao distinguishes, in his commentary on the *Sūtra of Meditations*, two kinds of devotional practice for the Nembutsu devotee, 'proper' and 'mixed'. The 'proper practice' consists in thinking (*nien*) of the name of the Buddha Amitābha with singleness of thought. But here too 'thinking of the name' has no meaning except when the name is deliberately pronounced. This kind of thinking is effective only when the vocal nerves and muscles are set in motion in accompaniment with the mental representation. In fact, it is doubtful whether any thinking, high or low, can be carried on without its muscular accompaniment, however slight and imperceptible it may be.

Adding to this psychological fact, the Pure Land philosophers propose the theory that the name (*nāmadheya*) is the repository of all the virtues belonging to the Buddha, that is to say, of all the inner attainments and virtues belonging to one Amitābha Buddha such as the fourfold knowledge, the triple body, the tenfold power, the fourfold fearlessness, etc. Together with all his external functions and virtues including his excellent features, his illuminating rays of light, his discourses on the Dharma, his deeds of salvation, etc.—they are all included in the name of the Buddha

Amitābha.[1] Thus, as we see further on, psychology and philosophy have combined to lay entire stress of the Nembutsu teaching on the pronouncement of the name.

In the *Wíjō-yōshyu* (Fas. II, Part 1), compiled by Genshin (942-1017), who was one of the forerunners of the Jōdo (Pure Land) school of Buddhism in Japan, the author raises the question: 'Is Nembutsu-samādhi to be gained by mere meditation or by vocal recitation?' The answer is given by a quotation from Chisha-daishi's *Maka-shikwan* (Chih-chê Tai-shih's *Mo-hê-chih-kuan*)[2] Fas. II, Part 1: 'Sometimes recitation and meditation go on hand in hand, sometimes meditation precedes and recitation follows, sometimes recitation comes first and then meditation. When recitation and meditation go on thus in constant succession and without interruption each thought as well as each sound is fixed on Amitābha.'[3] In this, the vocal Nembutsu is not yet brought out sufficiently prominently.

It was Hōnen (1133-1212) who, following the teaching of Shan-tao, emphasized the Nembutsu; that is, the recitation of the Buddha's name. This was regarded as the most important practice in the Pure Land school when the devotees wished to be re-born in the Land of Amida. Praising his virtues, making offerings, bowing before him, reading the sutras, and meditating on him—these were by no means to be slighted, but the chief act of piety consisted

---

[1] From Hōnen's *Passages Relative to the Nembutsu and Original Vows* (*Senjyaku nembutsu-hongwanshu*), Fas. I. In this Hōnen attempts to explain his position as founder of the Nembutsu school in Japan.

[2] The Taisho Tripitaka, No. 1911.

[3] Soon after this, Genshin quotes another authority in the Jōdo teaching, Huai-kan: 'According to the *Sūtra of the Meditations*, this one harassed to the extreme has no time to think of the Buddha; but being advised by good friends he recites the name of the Buddha Amitābha, and thereby he is enabled to keep up his recitation uninterruptedly and with sincerity of heart.—In a similar manner, let those who wish to attain a Samādhi in the Nembutsu keep up their recitation audibly without stopping, and they will surely realize the Samādhi and see the holy congregation of the Buddhas right before them as in the daylight.— The louder you recite the name of the Buddha at the top of your voice the easier the attainment of the Samādhi of the Nembutsu. When your recitation is not loud enough, the mind is liable to distraction. This will be found out by the Yogin himself without being told by others.'

in the recitation (ch'êng-ming). By constantly uttering his name with devotion, in whatever posture one may be in, whether sitting or standing, lying down or walking, he will surely, after some time has elapsed, be taken by Amida into his abode of happiness. For this, according to the masters of the Jōdo school, is in full accordance with the teachings of the sūtras; that is to say, with the original vows of the Buddha.

To confirm this view, Hōnen again quotes Shan-tao, according to whom the Nembutsu is easier to practise than any other deeds of devotion. The question as to why meditation is set aside in preference to singleminded recitation is answered thus: 'It is because sentient beings are all very heavily handicapped with hindrances, and the world in which they are living is full of subtle temptations; it is because their mind is too disconcerted, and their intelligence too clumsy, and their spirit too wandering. Meditation, therefore, is not theirs. Taking pity on them, the Buddha advises them to concentrate on reciting his name, for when this is practised without interruption the devotee is sure of his rebirth in the Land of Amida.'

Hōnen then proceeds to state that thinking or meditating is reciting, the two being the same; that to think of Amida is to recite his name and vice versa. Nembutsu, 'thinking of the Buddha', has thus come to be completely identified with shōmyō, 'reciting or pronouncing the name'; meditation has turned into recitation. What may be termed the Buddhist philosophy of nominalism has come to occupy the minds of the Pure Land devotees, for they now realize the presence in the name of something that goes altogether beyond conception. My object is now to study the psychological signification of this vocal Nembutsu and to see in what relationship it stands to the koan exercise as practised by followers of Zen.

4. The Psychology of the Shōmyō Exercise, and Where it Becomes Related to the Koan Exercise

With the vocalization of the Nembutsu on the one hand, Hōnen and his predecessors have not forgotten on the other hand to emphasize the importance and necessity of a believing heart. Meditating on the Buddha, as one in possession of all the virtuous qualities and also of the thirty-two marks of a great being, requires no doubt a great deal of concentration and may be beyond the psychic powers of an ordinary man. Compared to that, the recitation of the name is indeed much easier.

A name is something like an algebraic symbol; as *a* or *b* or *c* may stand for any kind of number, the name Amida may be regarded as representing everything that is contained in the conception of the Buddha, not only of one Amida, but of all the Buddhas, whose number is beyond calculation. When a man pronounces this name he digs down deeply into the content of his religious consciousness. Mere utterance, however, will be of no consequence, being devoid of sense; the uttering must be the outcome of deep thinking, earnest seeking, and great faith; if it is not the outcome of such intense yearnings, it must be strengthened continuously by them. Lips and heart must be in full accord in its practice.

In this kind of Nembutsu the mind focusses itself on the name and not on the outward form of the Buddha. His thirty-two physical marks of greatness are not pictured out in the mind of the devotee. The name possesses the entire field of consciousness. So we read in the *Smaller Sukhā-vativyūha* :[1] *amitāyuṣas tathāgatasya nāmadheyam śroṣyati śrutvā ca manasikariṣyati.* . . . (Let him hear the name of the Tathā-gata Amitāyus and, having heard it, keep it in mind. . . .)

The Chinese translator has *chih-ch'ih* for *manasikṛi*, meaning 'to hold an object of thought fixedly in mind'. The name itself is held at the centre of attention, not mere lip

[1] *Anecdota Oxoniensia*, Aryan series, Vol. I, Part II, p. 96.

repetition but an utterance of the heart. There is no doubt
that this kind of Nembutsu is a great help to concentration.
The calling-up of the form of the Buddha is pregnant with
many psychological dangers or evils, and the devotee may
become an incurable victim of hallucinations. The vocalization is a great step forward to the attainment of a true
religious Samādhi.

The object of the Nembutsu, we see clearly, has gone
through modifications. In the beginning it was remembering
the Buddha, longing to see him again as he had lived among
his followers—a desire entirely human and natural. Later,
it came to mean the coming into the presence of an
idealized Buddha, eternally living in the Land of Purity
and Happiness. And, finally, by holding the name firmly in
mind the explicit object became a desire to turn the
gracious attention of the Buddha towards the sinful devotee.
This modification is thus interpreted by masters of the Pure
Land school to be in full accord with the teaching of the
Buddha as expounded in the various sūtras belonging to
that school.

But the question that arises here is: Is there no psychological background which elicits this gradual modification? Has the vocal Nembutsu no implicit object? Has
it no other object than to direct the devotee to the Pure
Land of Amida? The masters might not have been conscious of the fact, but was there not a psychological experience on their part which made them teach the simple
vocal Nembutsu instead of other religious deeds, such as
sūtra-reading, meditating on the Buddha, making bows to
him, or singing hymns of praise?

If moral or spiritual enhancement is to be achieved, the
mere uttering of the name, even though it be the name of
the Holiest One, does not seem to elevate the mind so much
as meditating on him and reading his sermons. The Pure
Land teachers honestly believed in the sutras when the
vocal Nembutsu was recommended. But as far as the sūtras
are concerned they teach many other things also, and, if
the teachers so desired, they could therein develop some

other teachings than the Nembutsu. For a sūtra or in fact any religious literature generally lends itself, according to the reader's personal experience, to varities of interpretation.

The development of the vocal Nembutsu, therefore, must be said to have its psychological ground, as well as its philosophical and religious ones. It was, of course, the philosophical side that chiefly and therefore consciously governed the religious consciousness of the teachers.

It would be against reason to assert that the psychology of the vocal Nembutsu is all that constitutes the foundation of the Pure Land teachings. For such conceptions as sin, the reality of suffering, and the all-embracing love of Amida, are also essential factors, but my present study is solely to analyse the psychological aspect of it.

To give a name is to discriminate; to discriminate is to recognize the reality of an individual object, and to make it accessible to the human understanding as well as to the human heart. Therefore, when the name is pronounced, we feel that the object itself is with us, and it was a most natural process of development that thinking of the Buddha gradually turned into pronouncing his name. But what we wish to examine now is that the name of the Buddha continued to retain its original Sanskrit form, or rather its transliteration, throughout its long history in China and Japan.

Why was not the Buddha addressed by the Chinese or Japanese equivalent instead of by the original or modified Sanskrit? *Namu amida butsu* and *Nan wu o mi to fo* are the Japanese and the Chinese way of reading *namo 'mitābhāya buddhāya*. *Namo* or *namas* means 'adoration' or 'salutation', and *amitābhāya buddhāya* means 'to the Buddha of Infinite Light', which in Chinese is *kuei i wu liang kuang fo*. Why did they not say 'Adoration to the Buddha of Infinite Light', instead of 'Namu Amida Butsu' or 'Nan-wu O-mi-to Fo'?

These transliterations give no sense ordinarily to the Japanese or Chinese mind, as they are modified Sanskrit sounds and apparently carry no meaning. It is to them a sort of Dhāraṇī or Mantram which is to be pronounced as it stands with no translation; for when translated a Dhāraṇī conveys no intelligent thought, being no more than a stream of jargon. What was the reason of this— intelligence giving way to non-intelligence, sense to non-sense, clearness to obscurity, discrimination to non-dis-crimination? Why, all the time, Namu Amida Butsu, Namu Amida Butsu?

In my view, the reason is to be sought not in the magical effect of the name itself, but in the psychological effect of its repetition. Wherever there is an intelligent meaning, it suggests an endless train of ideas and feelings attached thereto; the mind then either becomes engaged in working a logical loom, or becomes inextricably involved in the meshes of imagination and association. When meaningless sounds are repeated, the mind stops there, not having chances to wander about. Images and hallucinations are less apt to invade it. To use Buddhist terminology, the external dust of discrimination covers the original bright surface of the inner mirror of enlightenment.

To avoid this tragedy, it is necessary that sounds in-tended for the vocal Nembutsu should be devoid of in-telligible meaning. When the reflective and the medita-tive Nembutsu developed into the vocal Nembutsu, there must have been some such psychological experience on the part of the masters who wanted to concentrate their minds on Buddhahood itself and not on the personality of the Buddha. The thought of the personality of the Buddha, as they saw it, demands a higher process of mentality and yet does not always yield genuine results.

The Jōdo masters are always quite emphatic on the triple attitude of mind which should always accompany the vocal Nembutsu: 1. Sincerity of heart; 2. Inwardness of faith; and 3. The desire for the Land of Amida. Without these subjective factors, indeed, no amount of Nembutsu will be of use to the devotee in gaining the object of his desire. But the masters in their apparently too earnest desire to propagate the so-called easy method of salvation, and to bring out in the strongest possible light the necessity of the vocal Nembutsu, seem sometimes to set aside the importance of these subjective conditions. As a result the students of the Pure Land schools are often attracted too irresistibly to the vocal Nembutsu at the expense of the right subjective conditions.

This is not right, but one may wonder whether there is not something in the attitude of the masters which will justify this erroneous assumption. Are they not emphasizing the importance of the subjective factors in order to make the vocal Nembutsu effective to its utmost extent? If a man had all these inner requirements fulfilled, it does not seem, as far as ordinary logic goes, to matter very much whether he was a devotee of sūtra-reading, or of bowings, or of the vocal Nembutsu. But the masters, especially of the Jōdo school of Genku and Hōnen, are unmistakably insistent on uttering the name of the Buddha in the form of 'Namu Amida Butsu' as the most essential practice, relegating all other devotional exercises to a secondary category. According to them, therefore, the 'Namu Amida Butsu' is what finally guarantees one's rebirth in the Land of Bliss.

How can this be so unless the vocal Nembutsu works in some mysterious manner in the consciousness of the devotee? When a certain state of consciousness is induced by repeatedly pronouncing the Buddha-name it is likely that the Buddha himself comes to take possession of the mind, whereby the devotee is assured of his future destiny. Was this psychology what was aimed at by Shan-tao, Hōnen, and other teachers of the Jōdo school?

When such great Jōdo teachers as Shan-tao, Tao-ch'o, and Huai-kan give two ways of rebirth in the Pure Land, (1) saying the Nembutsu and (2) practising other meritorious deeds, and prefer the first to the second as being more in accord with the teachings of the sūtras, and further when they identify 'thinking of' or 'meditating on' (*nien* in Chinese, *anusmṛiti* in Sanskrit) with 'voicing' or 'uttering' (*shêng*), saying that to think of Buddha is to utter his name, do they find this reason for identification in logic or in psychology? Logically, to think intensely of an object does not necessarily mean uttering its name; the thinking is independent of the uttering of its name; the thinking is independent of the uttering especially when the mind meditatively dwells on an object of devotion and reverence. But as a matter of psychological fact, the thinking of abstract ideas is greatly helped by looking at some graphical representations, letters, or diagrams, and also by pronouncing names mentally or audibly. Grounded on this psychological fact, they must have come to the conclusion that thinking of the Buddha is uttering his name, that the thinking and the uttering are identical.

And again, according to Huai-kan's commentary[1] on the noted passage in the *Tai-chi yüeh-tsang Ching*:[2] 'By great thinking (*nien*) one sees great Buddha, and by small thinking, small Buddha. Great thinking means calling out the Buddha [-name] at a high pitch; small thinking at a low pitch.' While I am not quite sure as to what is exactly meant by 'seeing great Buddha and small Buddha', it is readily seen that the teachers are here making much of saying the Nembutsu loudly. The more muscular effort we make in uttering the name of the Buddha the higher degree of concentration will be attained, and thus the holding in mind of 'Namu Amida Butsu' will be the more effective.

Whatever doctrinal interpretations were given to the fact, the teachers must have had some psychological experience before they confirmed the identification of thinking (*nien*) and uttering (*shêng*). Do we not see here something of Zen psychology in which ' "Wu", "*Wu*", all day today, and "*Wu*", "*Wu*", over again all day tomorrow',[3] is practised? Hence their exhortation to say the Nembutsu all day, or every day regularly, or so many times a day—ten thousand times, fifty thousand, and even up to a hundred thousand times a day. There is a Jōdo temple in Kyoto, the

---

[1] Quoted by Hōnen in his *Senjaku-shu*, Fas. I.

[2] *Candra-garbha*, translated into Chinese by Narendrayaśas, A.D. 550–577.

[3] In one of Kung-ku Lung's letters.

name of which is 'One Million Times', referring to the number of the vocal Nembutsu to be repeated. The mental fact that vocalization helps concentration is the basis of the doctrine of the vocal Nembutsu (*shōmyō*, or *shêng-ming*).

When the Buddha-name is so frequently repeated as ten or twenty thousand times at a stretch, the practice grows mechanical with no conscious effort, therefore with no conscious realization of the three factors of devotion. Is this mechanization to be considered the effective means of the rebirth? Is there no need of the devotee's making a determined effort to grow up in his belief and devotion? Does this constant muttering or uttering of meaningless sounds produce in the consciousness of the devotee a definite sense of assurance whereby he cherishes no doubt as to his rebirth in the Pure Land, or as to his salvation through the grace of Amida?

When the Nembutsu is turned into pronouncing a Dhāraṇī without any conscious reference to its meaning, literary and devotional, its psychological effect will be to create a state of unconsciousness in which ideas and feelings superficially floating are wiped off. Morally speaking, this is a condition of innocence as there is no discrimination of good and bad, and in this way the Jōdo teachers state that the Nembutsu wipes off all the sins accumulated during one's lives in countless past ages.

The perpetual reiteration of 'Namu Amida Butsu'[1] has its parallel in Sufism whose followers repeat the name 'Allah', as has been observed by R. A. Nicholson in his *Studies in Islam Mysticism*, 'as a method practised by Moslem mystics for bringing about *fana*, i.e. the passing away from self, or in Pascals' phrase, *"oubli du monde et de tout hormis Dieu"*.'[2]

We cannot think that the mere repetition of 'Namu Amida Butsu' assures the devotee of his rebirth in the Pure Land in spite of all the guarantee that is given in the sutras

---

[1] In the practical recitation, this is pronounced something like *nam man da bu, nam man da bu,* . . .

[2] Pp. 7–9.

and by the teachers of that school, unless the reiteration produces a certain mental effect wherein he attains the realization by himself. And is not this realization what is known as the Samādhi of Nembutsu or the Samādhi of Oneness (*ekavyūha*)?

In the *Anrakushu* (*An-lê-chi*, Part II) by Tao-ch'o, the passages bearing on this Samādhi are quoted from various sūtras. The author's intention here is to prove the Samādhi to be the efficient means of bringing the devotee into the presence of all the Buddhas of the past, present, and future. But, from the point of view of salvation (or enlightenment), what is the use of seeing the Buddhas unless their assurance of salvation evokes the sense of its truth in the consciousness of the devotee? The seeing of the Buddha objectively must be in correspondence with the inner realization and, as far as psychology is concerned, inner realization is the more important topic of consideration.

There is a sūtra entitled *Bosatsu Nembutsu Sammai* (*samādhi*) *Kyo*, first translated by Dharmagupta of Sui, in which all the necessary instructions concerning the practice of the Nembutsu Samādhi are given in detail. According to this work, the chief merit accruing from the Samādhi seems to be the realization of supreme enlightenment. Evidently the coming into the presence of all the Buddhas is not to see them in their company as spiritually enlightened beings, to be in communion with them in a world transcending all forms of corporeality. The devotee is persuaded to practise the Nembutsu in order to see the Buddhas, but when he actually enters into a Samādhi he sees them in a way quite different from what he might have expected in the beginning.[1]

Hōnen quotes in his *Senjakushu*, Part II, a passage from *Lives of the Pious Followers of the Pure Land School*, in which reference is made to Shan-tao's attainment of the Samādhi. According to this account, the Samādhi among other things seems to give one a prophetic insight into the spiritual condition of others; for the account reveals that Shan-tao

[1] Cf. Hakuin's story of the two Jōdo devotees told below, p. 184.

could tell about the past lives of his own teacher, Tao-ch'o, and also about the rebirth of the latter in the Land of Amida.

By the fact that the Samādhi could not go any farther than the attainment of these miraculous powers, we may say that it has not much to do with one's spiritual enhancement and assurance of emancipation. There must be something more in the Samādhi acquired by means of the Nembutsu. The teachers of the Pure Land school have been too eager to advance their religious views regarding rebirth after death, ignoring the psychological effect which is sure to follow the constant reiteration of 'Namu Amida Butsu'. They have been too busy reminding us of this degenerate age in which the pure form of Buddhism is too difficult to maintain itself, and, therefore, that the uttering of the Buddha-name is the best, easiest, and surest for beings of this degenerate age to come into the presence of the Buddhas and to be embraced in the arms of their infinite love.

In this respect, Shinran pushed this idea to its utmost logical end; for he states in connection with one's rebirth in the Pure Land by uttering the name of the Buddha only ten times that 'this does not mean to specifically and quietly meditate on the Buddha, or to think of him intensely, but merely to pronounce the name'. With all their expostulations about the Nembutsu, about saying it once or up to ten times, which will surely be heard by the Buddha, I cannot imagine that the teachers were utterly unconscious of the psychology of the Nembutsu, as has already been referred to.

5. *What is the Object of the Nembutsu Exercise?*

One may ask in this connection: Whatever the content of the Samādhi, which is the real object of the Nembutsu, rebirth in the Pure Land or the Samādhi itself? Or is the Samādhi a kind of foretaste of the rebirth? No teachers of the Jōdo as far as I can learn make this point thoroughly clear for us. But if we can so view the matter, the Samādhi may be regarded as the subjective and psychological aspect of the Nembutsu exercise, and the rebirth as the objective and ontological aspect.

In this case, the Samādhi and the rebirth are only the same thing described in two ways, but as the Samādhi is attainable in this life while rebirth is an affair taking place after death, the Samādhi must be said to be identical with the rebirth in a most specific sense; that is, the rebirth is not to be judged as an objective and temporal event, but as a form of subjective assurance of a thing that is surely to take place. If so, the rebirth means a spiritual regeneration and as such it can be regarded as identical with the Samādhi.

This view of the Samādhi is supported in the *Anjin Ketsujōshō* by an unknown author, which is, however, one of the most significant books on the teaching of the Jōdo school. In this the author states that the faith is to be firmly established by the realization of the Samādhi—the faith in the original vow of Amida whereby the devotee is assured of his future destiny. For the Samādhi obtains when the mind of the devotee is so perfectly identified with the mind of Amida that the consciousness of the dualism is altogether effaced from it. This conclusion, not only in logic but from the factual point of view, is inevitable seeing that the entire structure of Buddhist philosophy is based on an idealistic monism, and no exception is to be made about the realistic Jōdo. Read this from the *Meditation Sūtra*:

'The Buddha said to Ānanda and Vaidehī: After you have seen these, you should think of the Buddha. You may ask, How? Every Buddha-Tathāgata has his body in the spiritual world (*dharmadhātu*) and enters into the mind of every sentient being. Therefore, when you think of the Buddha, your mind itself becomes endowed with the thirty-two marks of greatness and also with the eighty secondary marks of excellence. This mind is transformed into Buddhahood, this mind is no other than the Buddha himself. The ocean of true all-knowledge possessed by the Buddhas grows out of your own mind and thought. For this reason, you should apply yourselves with singleness of thought to meditation on the Buddha-Tathāgata, who is an Arhat and a Fully-enlightened One.'

In the *Pratyutpannasamādhi Sūtra*,[1] which is thought by the Jōdo teachers to be one of the sources of their teachings, we have this:

'And again, Bhadrapāla, when a young man of fine mien wishes to see his own features, ugly or handsome, he takes up a vessel of refined oil or of clean water, or he brings out a crystal or a mirror. When either one of these four objects reflects his image in it, he definitely knows how he looks, ugly or handsome. Bhadrapāla, do you think that what the young man sees in these four objects has been already in existence there?

'Answered Bhadrapāla, O no, Blessed One.

'Is it to be regarded altogether as a non-entity?

'O no, Blessed One.

'Is it to be regarded as being within them?

'O no, Blessed One.

'Is it to be regarded as outside them?

'O no, Blessed One. As the oil and water and crystal and mirror are clear, transparent, and free from muddiness and dust, the image is reflected in them when a person stands before them. The image does not come out of the object, nor does it get into them from the outside, nor is it there by itself, nor is it artificially constructed. The image comes from nowhere, vanishes away to nowhere; it is not subject to birth and death; it has no fixed abode.

'When Bhadrapāla finished thus answering, the Buddha said:

'Bhadrapāla, so it is, indeed, as you say. When the

---

[1] Translated into Chinese for the first time by Chih Lou-chia-ch'ien, who came to China in the latter half of the second century, during the latter Han dynasty. The English translation is drawn from Jñānagupta's Chinese translation (A.D. 586), instead of from Chih Lou-chai-ch'ien (A.D. 179); for Jñānagupta's is more intelligible, though Chih Lou-chia-ch'ien is better known to students of the Pure Land school. The Taisho Tripitaka, Nos. 416–419.

objects are pure and clean, the image is reflected in them without much trouble. So is it with the Bodhisattva. When he meditates on the Buddhas with singleness of thought, he sees them; having appeared to him they stay with him; staying with him, they explain things to him that he wishes to understand. Being thus enlightened by them he is delighted; he now reflects: Whence do these Buddhas come? And whither does this body of mine vanish? When he thus reflects he sees that all the Tathāgatas come from nowhere and go out nowhere. So it is with my own body; it has no definite path by which it comes, and how can there be any returning to anywhere?

'He reflects again: This triple world exists only because of the mind. According to one's own thought, one sees oneself in one's own mind. My now seeing the Buddha is after my own mind; my mind becomes the Buddha; my mind itself is the Buddha; my mind itself is the Tathāgata. My mind is my body, my mind sees the Buddha; the mind does not know itself, the mind does not see itself. When thoughts are stirred, there is Nirvāna. All things have no reality in themselves, they take their rise owing to thought and laws of origination. When that which is thought vanishes, the thinking one himself vanishes. Bhadrapāla, you should know that all the Bodhisattvas by means of this Samādhi attained great enlightenment.'

Viewing the Samādhi of Nembutsu from this absolute idealistic point of view—the Samādhi that is realized by constant reiteration of 'Namu Amida Butsu'—we can state that the Samādhi, and the establishment of faith in the Buddha, and the assurance of rebirth in his Land of Purity, describe one and the same psychological fact which constitutes the foundation of the Jōdo (Pure Land) doctrine.

Hōnen says in his commentary on the *Meditation Sūtra* that the devotee should be like a man who has lost his senses, or like a deaf and dumb person, or like an idiot, when he devotes himself exclusively to the practice of the Nembutsu, pronouncing the name of the Buddha day and night, whether sitting or standing, lying down or walking, and for any length of time, one day, two days, a week, a month, a year, or even two or three years. When the practice is carried on in such wise, the devotee will surely some day attain the Samādhi and have his Dharma-eye opened, and he will view a world that is altogether beyond thought and imagination. This is 'a mysterious realm where all thoughts cease and all imaginings are swept away, being in full correspondence with a state of Samādhi'.

In this Samādhi where the devotee is fully confirmed in the faith, according to the author of the *Anjin Ketsujōshō*, 'The body becomes "Namu Amida Butsu", and the mind becomes "Namu Amida Butsu".' If so, is this not a mystic state of consciousness corresponding to that which is realized by the koan exercise?

The explicit claim made by the Jōdo teachers, that the repetition of the Nembutsu is the easiest method of salvation for all beings, is of course based on the original vow of Amida, in which the Buddha assures his followers of their rebirth in his Land of Bliss, if they only pronounce his name as showing their good faith and willingness to be thus saved.

To re-enforce or strengthen their teaching, they describe, on the one hand, in glowing terms the beauties of the Pure Land, while, on the other hand, they are never tired of picturing the miseries and horrors of this world, and the sinfulness and the helpless ignorance of the beings therein. Therefore, those who wish to be helped by this doctrine will have to be earnest devotees of 'Namu Amida Butsu' and be pronouncing and reciting the phrase all the time. But when they are doing this, their ultimate object of being members of the Pure Land community may gradually give way to the immediate daily practice itself of the Nembutsu. And even when their deliberate attention is focussed upon it, the psychology of the unconscious may begin to function by itself independently of the ultimate aim, which is supposed to take place at the end of this life; for the nearer happenings always claim the more intimate and intense concentration of mind.

Let this concentration be brought up to the highest pitch and there will be the intuition of such mystical truths as these: Rebirth is no-birth; to think of Buddha is not to have any thought; every moment is the last; this mind is no other than the Tathāgata himself; while the body belongs to this world, the mind is enjoying itself in the Pure Land; this body, as it is, is of the same order as Maitreya Bodhisattva, etc. Such statements seem to be not so typically Jōdo; in fact they go much against its generally realistic tendency, but we cannot altogether ignore this mysticism entering into the structural foundations of practical Jōdo, and there is no doubt that this comes from the psychology of the Nembutsu.

The Shin Branch of the Pure Land sect emphasizes faith as the only condition of rebirth in the land of Amida. Absolute trust is placed in the wisdom of the Buddha which goes altogether beyond human conception. Put, therefore, your faith in this wonder-working wisdom of Amida and you will straightway be taken up by him; there is no need for your waiting for the last moment when a band of welcoming Buddhas comes down from above; nor need you entertain any anxious fears about your destiny after death, thinking whether or not you are after all bound for Naraka (hell). All that is required of you is to abandon all thoughts regarding yourself and to put your unconditioned trust in the Buddha who knows best how to look after your welfare.[1] You need not worry at all about the last hour when you have to bid farewell to this life on earth. If, while living, you had been instructed by a wise adviser and had awakened one thought of trust in the Buddha, that moment of awakening was for you the last moment on earth. When trusting the original vow of Amida 'Namu Amida Butsu' is once pronounced, you are assured of rebirth in his Land; for this believing heart is the rebirth.[2]

But how can one really have this believing heart which

[1] *Shūji-shō.*
[2] From *Yui-shin Shō Mon-i.*

raises the owner at once to the order of the fully-enlightened One, bringing him up to the company even of Maitreya?[1] Mere listening to the teachers will not do it. Nor will the mere saying of the Nembutsu. How does one come to have this absolute faith—the faith which is evidently the same in substance as enlightenment? How can we be sure of our rebirth? How do we come to entertain no doubts as to our future destiny?

A certain state of consciousness must be awakened within us whereby we can be confirmed in our faith. Reasoning, or reading the sūtras, or listening to the discourses of the wise and enlightened will not induce this consciousness. As the history of religions tells us, there must be an intuitive insight into the truth, which is the abandoning of the self into the original vow of Amida. And is not this the moment when 'Namu Amida Butsu' gushes out of one's inmost heart (*adhyāśaya*)? Is this not what the Shin teachers mean when they say, 'Utter the Name once, and you are saved'?

6. *Mysticism of the Nembutsu, and the Uttering of the Name*

When we thus interpret the Nembutsu, we are able to understand the discourse of Ippen:[2] 'The rebirth means the first awakening of thought, and this assumes an existence, i.e. one in whom a thought is awakened. The "Namu Amida Butsu" itself is the rebirth, and the rebirth is no-birth. When this realization takes place, I call it provisionally the first awakening of thought. When one is absorbed in the Buddha-name that is above time, there is the rebirth that knows no beginning, no end.

'Sometimes the distinction is made between the last moment of life and everyday life, but this is a teaching that is based on confused thought. In the "Namu Amida Butsu"

---

[1] Op. cit.
[2] The founder of the Ji sect of the Pure Land school, 1229–1289. His *Sayings* is full of mystic thoughts.

itself there is no last moment, no everyday life; it is a reality abiding through all periods of time. As regards human life, it is a series of moments lasting only between an in-breath and an out-breath, and therefore the very moment of thought is the last moment of life. If so, every thought-moment is the last moment and every moment is a rebirth.'

The meaning of this mystical utterance by Ippen will become more transparent when the following quotations are gone through. 'When one's mind (or consciousness) is all annulled by saying "Namu Amida Butsu", this is the right thought for the last moment.' 'There is the Buddha-name only, and beyond it there is neither the one who says it, nor the one to whom it is addressed. There is the Buddha-name only, and beyond it there is no rebirth. All things existent are virtues included within the body of the Buddha-name itself. If so, when you attain the perception of all things as unborn, where all traces of a conscious mind vanish, saying "Namu Amida Butsu", a first thought then awakened is called the right thought of one's last moment; for this is no other than the thought of enlightenment, which is "Namu Amida Butsu".'

'Rather be possessed by the name than be possessing the name. All things are of one mind, but this mind is not manifested by itself. The eye cannot see itself, the wood cannot burn itself though it is by nature combustible. But hold a mirror before yourself and the eye can see itself—this is the virtue of the mirror. And the mirror is the one owned by every one of us and is known as the Great Mirror of Enlightenment; it is the name already realized by all the Buddhas. This being so, see your own original features in the Mirror of Enlightenment. Do we not read in the *Meditation Sūtra* that it is like seeing one's own face in the mirror?

'Again, wood will be burned when ignited by fire—the fire that burns is identical with the fire that is latent in the wood. It is thus through the concordance of causes inner and outer that all things are brought into actual existence. Though we are all endowed with the Buddha-nature, this of itself does not burn up the passions unless it be enkindled by the fire of transcendental wisdom which is the name (*nāmadheya*). The Jōdo school teaches that to take hold of an object one has to get away from it. The injunction is to be called to mind in this connection.'

Literally, 'Namu Amida Butsu' is not the name (*nāmadheya*) itself; it contains more than that, because *namu* (*namas* in Sanskrit) means 'adoration' or 'salutation'; but generally the whole phrase, 'Namu Amida Butsu', is regarded as the name, and its mysterious working is extolled. The masters of the Pure Land school exhausted their philosophical ingenuity on the subject, but strangely they keep quiet about the psychological aspect of the experience. Perhaps this silence comes from their conception of Amida, which is fundamentally ontological. But when it is asserted that the name alone exists and thus in it vanishes the dualistic contrast of the one who reiterates it and the one to whom it is addressed, this is the statement of a mystical experience and not of metaphysical reflection. The experience arising from the utterance of the name is of the same nature as that which ensues from the koan exercise. When the objective aspect of the experience is metaphysically interpreted, the name is objectified and Amida is absolute 'other-power'; but, on the other hand, let the devotee be a follower of Zen, and his understanding of it will be thoroughly idealistic.

The author of the *Anjin Ketsujōshō* may also, like Ippen, be considered an emphatic upholder of the name, for he says: 'As there is not a moment's separation between the devotee who says "Namu" and Amida-butsu himself, every thought cherished by him is "Namu Amida Butsu". This being so, every breath of his has never even for a moment been separated from the virtues of the Buddha; his whole being, indeed, is the substance of "Namu Amida Butsu". . . . When there is an understanding as to the meaning of the Nembutsu-Samādhi, both his body and his mind are "Namu Amida Butsu".

M

'For that reason, when all beings of the past, present, and future raise one thought of faith [in the original vow of Amida], the very thought goes back to the one thought of Enlightenment [which was originally awakened in the Buddha]; and the minds of all sentient beings in the ten quarters, when they utter the name, also go back to the one thought of Enlightenment. No thought, no utterance ever issuing from the devotees remains with them [they all go back to the source whence comes Enlightenment]. As the original vow is an act in which the name and essence are synthesized, the name contains in itself the whole essence of Enlightenment, and as it is thus the essence of Enlightenment, it is rebirth on the part of all beings in the ten quarters.'

Whether the masters of the Jōdo school, including the Shin, are conscious of the fact or not, there is something distinctly psychological in their metaphysical conclusions, or in their theology if that term could be used in Buddhism. Psychology cannot be said to be everything in religion, though it constitutes the groundwork of it. Thus even in Shin, where faith is made the chief principle of its teachings, there are many statements of Shinran, its founder, which are unintelligible unless his mystical experience is taken into consideration.

For instance, when he teaches the identity of the name and the original vow in their going beyond human understanding, he bases it on the Buddha's teaching itself. The explanation is simple enough, but how do we get confirmed in our belief? Especially when the masters of Shin all exhort us to abandon learning and reasoning, how can we accept everything that is poured into our heads rather mechanically; that is, on what authority? Some psychological state must come to us, even to the most unlogical minds, that leads us to say 'yes' to all that is told us to believe. Why is the name to be pronounced in addition to believing in the vow? It may be that the pronouncing is the believing and *vice versa*, but this identification, too, must be an outcome of experience and not a logical inference.

'The vow and the name are not two separate things, for there is no name apart from the vow, nor is there any vow apart from the name. Even making this statement involves human understanding. When, believing in the vow as beyond the understanding and also in the name as beyond the understanding, you utter the name in oneness of thought, why should you exercise your own understanding?'[1]

The believing alone seems to be sufficient to guarantee a man's rebirth in the Pure Land, or in Enlightenment, and why should this uttering the name be considered essential too? There is no uttering the name, it is declared, separate from the faith, and also there is no believing thought disjoined from the name; but why such importance given to the name? Why is 'Namu Amida Butsu' so essential to the confirmation of faith?

The name, whose meaning consists in having no meaning as it transcends the relativity of human knowledge, must be once demonstrated in experience before one realizes that it is really so. 'Namu Amida Butsu', from the Zen point of view, is a koan given to followers of the Pure Land school. One day the mystery of the name is realized as it is uttered, and this is the moment when the key is delivered into the hand of the devotee, to whom the entire treasure of religious consciousness is now safely entrusted.

'The original vow of Amida is to welcome anybody to his Land of Bliss who should utter his name in absolute confidence; being so, blessed are those who utter the name. A man may have the faith, but if he utters not the name, his faith will be of no avail. Another may utter the name singlemindedly, but if his faith is not deep enough his rebirth will not take place. He, however, who firmly believes in the rebirth as the outcome of the Nembutsu and utters the name, will doubtless be reborn in the Land of Recompense.'[2]

It can readily be understood that without faith rebirth

[1] *Mattōsho*. This is a collection of Shinran's letters, twenty-three in all.
[2] *The Mattōsho*.

is impossible, but why the uttering of the name? To comprehend this mystery, which constitutes the transcendental wisdom of all the Buddhas, the depths of our own being must be penetrated, and there is no doubt, according to the Jōdo, that it is the 'Namu Amida Butsu' which fathoms these depths.

7. *Experience and Theorization*

All religion is built upon the foundation of mystical experience, without which all its metaphysical or theological superstructure collapses. This is where religion differs from philosophy. All the philosophical systems may some day be found in ruins, but the religious life will for ever go on experiencing its deep mysteries. The Jōdo and the Zen cannot separate themselves from these mysteries. The Jōdo bases its theory on the Nembutsu and the Zen bases theirs on the koan exercise. As far as their theoretical edifices are concerned they seem very dissimilar to each other.

The Jōdo wants to see its followers reborn in the Land of Bliss and there attain their enlightenment. To do this they are taught about their sinfulness, about their intellectual inabilities to grasp the higher truths of Buddhism, and also about their being too heavily laden by their past karma to shake themselves free of their shackles by their own limited efforts. Amida is now held up before them, whose original vow is to give them a helping hand for crossing the stream of birth and death. But this helping hand cannot be reached unless they utter the name of their saviour with singleness of thought (*ekacitta*).

To awaken this state of singlemindedness, that is, 'one thought of faith', as it is technically termed, is the great problem of the Jōdo teaching. The vow, the name, the 'one thought of faith', the uttering of the name, the rebirth— these are the links making up the chain of the Pure Land doctrine. When any one of these links is held fast the entire chain will be in your hand, and the masters of the Jōdo have set up the uttering of the name in the most prominent position. In this the Jōdo experience is the counterpart of the Zen experience. The vocal Nembutsu and the koan exercise are here standing on a common ground.

Psychologically considered, the aim of the vocal Nembutsu is to do away with the fundamental dualism which is a condition of our empirical consciousness. By achieving this the devotee rides over the theoretical difficulties and contradictions that have troubled him before. With all intensity of thought and will (*adhyāsana*) he has thrown himself into the deeps of his own being. He is not, however, a mere wanderer without anything to guide him, for he has the name with him. He walks along with it, he goes down to the abyss with it; though he finds himself frequently divorced from it, he always remembers it and keeps in its company.

One day, without knowing how, he is no more himself, nor is he with the name. The name alone there is, and he is the name, the name is he. Suddenly even this disappears, which is not a state of mental blankness or of total unconsciousness. All these psychological designations fail to describe the state of mind in which he now is. But he stays not even here, for he awakes from it as suddenly as before. As he awakes, he awakes with a thought, which is the name and the faith in the original vow of Amida and the rebirth. This emerging from a state of absolute identity is marked with the utterance of 'Namu Amida Butsu', because he comes to this awakening through the teaching of his school.

Religion is fundamentally a personal experience, but the intellect enters into every fibre of the faith thus realized. For when the experience receives its name, that is, when it comes to be designated as faith, it has already gone through the baptism of intellection. Though the latter in itself is powerless, it gains authority as soon as it is combined with the experience. Thus we find almost all religious controversies centering about the philosophy of the experience; in other words, about theological subtleties and not about the experience itself. How to interpret the experience thus

becomes frequently the cause of a most irreligious per-
secution or the bloodiest warfare.

However this may be, the religious experience always
remains the sustaining and driving energy of its metaphysical system. This explains the diversity of intellectual
interpretations even within one body of Buddhism, the one as
Zen and the other as Jōdo, while their experience remains
as far as psychology is concerned fundamentally the same.

This also explains the historical connection that came to
exist between Zen and Jōdo. Superficially or intellectually
observed, take for instance one of the numerous Zen koans
and compare it with the 'Namu Amida Butsu'. How utterly
unrelated they appear! 'What is it that stands for ever
companionless?' 'I'll tell you when you have swallowed up
in one draught all the waves of the Hsi!' 'What was Bodhidharma's idea in coming from the West?' 'The eastern
mountains move over the waves.'

Between these koans and 'Namu Amida Butsu' there is
no possible relationship as far as their appeal to the intellect is concerned. 'Namu Amida Butsu', as literally meaning 'Adoration to Amitābha Buddha', is intelligible enough;
but as to the mountains moving over the waves, or one swal-
lowing a whole river in one draught, there is no intelligible
sense; all we can say about them is 'nonsense!' How can
these nonsensical utterances be related to the Nembutsu?

As was explained above, however, the Nembutsu ceased
to mean 'meditating on the Buddha' and came to be
identified with the name (ming-hao), or rather with 'uttering
the name' (ch'êng-ming). Meditation, or 'coming into the
presence of the Buddha', thus gave way to the constant
reiteration of the phrase as not always or necessarily referring to any definite objective reality, but merely as a
name somehow beyond comprehension, or rather as a
symbol standing for something indescribable, unpredictable,
altogether transcending the intellect, and therefore sug-
gesting a meaning beyond meaning.

When the Nembutsu comes to this, the name closely
approaches the koan. Hitherto the Nembutsu and the koan

exercise have been walking down their different routes of historical development, but now they find themselves near each other, and, as they look at each other, each most unexpectedly recognizes himself in the other.

Zen wants to clear one's consciousness of all its intellectual sediments so that it can receive the first awakening of thought in its purity, in its unaffected simplicity; for this purpose the koan, which is devoid of sense as ordinarily understood, is given to its followers. The idea is to go back to the original blankness in which there was as yet no functioning consciousness. This is a state of no-birth. Zen starts from it and so does the Jōdo.

8. *Hakuin's View on Koan and Nembutsu*

By way of conclusion, let me quote the following, which is a part of a letter[1] written by Hakuin to one of his noblemen followers, and in which he discusses the relative merit of the Nembutsu and the koan as instrumental in bringing about the state of satori. Hakuin does not slight the value of Nembutsu or Shōmyō, which is practically the same in the minds of the Pure Land followers, but he thinks the koan exercise is far more effective in that it intensely awakens the spirit of inquiry in the Zen Yogin's mind, and it is this spirit that finally rises up to the Zen experience. The Nembutsu may also achieve this, but only accidentally and in some exceptional cases; for there is nothing inherent in Nembutsu which would stir up the spirit of inquiry.

Hakuin also cites examples of some Nembutsu devotees who attained thereby a satori. Let us begin with this citation:

During the Genroku period (1688–1703) there were two such Buddhists, the one was called Yenjo and the other Yengu. After the realization Yenjo saw Dokutan, the Zen master, who asked, 'Where is your native land?'

[1] From a booklet known as the *Orategama* which is a collection of some of his letters. The work is read very much by his followers.

'Yamashiro,' was the answer.

'What is your faith?'

'The Pure Land.'

'What is the age of Amida?'

'Of the same age as myself.'

'What is yours?'

'Same as that of Amida.'

'Where is he now?' Dokutan demanded.

Yenjo closed the left hand a little and raised it.

Dokutan was surprised to see this and said, 'You are a real follower of the Nembutsu.'[1]

Later on, Yengu also attained realization.

There was another man about the same time who was called Sokuwo, also a Nembutsu devotee. By virtue of his singleminded practice, he was also enabled to realize the truth of Buddhism. Hakuin writes that he himself has recorded these facts elsewhere.

Hakuin was, we can thus see, by no means an exclusive upholder of the Zen exercise, but he did not wish to see his Zen followers diverted from their regular discipline. The letter further reads:

'When I say that the "*Mu*" (*wu*) and the Myōgō (*nāmadheya*, or Buddha-name, or Nembutsu) are of the same order, I must not forget to mention that there is some difference between the two as regards the time of final experience and the depth of intuition. For those Zen students of the highest capacity who wish to stop up the leakage of dualistic imaginations and to remove the cataract of ignorance, nothing compares to the effectiveness of the "*Mu*". So we read in the verse of Fa-yen of Wu-tsu Shan:

> ' "Chao-chou's sword blade is out of its scabbard,
> How cold like frost, how blazing like a flame!
> If one attempts to ask 'How so?'
> A division at once sets in—this and that."

[1] Shuo-shan Shih-chieh was asked by a general, 'What is the age of Shuo-shan?' 'Same as vacuity of space.' 'What is the age of space?' 'Same as Shuo-shan.' *The Transmission of the Lamp*, XI. (Here Hakuin describes the psychological state of the Zen Yogin who practises the '*Mu*' exercise. This was already quoted on p. 131.)

'At this supreme moment [of Zen experience], Nirvāṇa and Saṁsāra are like a dream of yesterday, and the ocean of worlds in the great chiliocosm appears like a bubble, and even all the holy ones of the past, present, and future are like the flashes of great lightning. This is the great moment of satori known as the occasion of *ho ti i hsia* (exclaiming "*Ho!*").[1]

'The experience is beyond description, and can never be transmitted to others. It is those who have actually drunk water that know whether it is cold or warm. The ten quarters are melted into the spot of your presence; the past, present, and future are concentrated in this moment of your consciousness. Even among the celestial beings no joy is ever comparable to this, much less among humankind. Such advancement in one's spiritual life can be acquired even in a few days, if only the Yogins are devoted enough to the exercise.

'How is it possible to stimulate a spirit of inquiry to a state of great fixation?

'Not necessarily avoiding moments of activity, nor specially favouring places of quietude, inquire into the meaning of the "*Mu*", saying to yourself that "This body of mine is the '*Mu*' itself, and what does it all mean?" Throw away all thoughts and imaginations, exclusively applying yourself to the "*Mu*"—what does it mean? What sense is there in it? When you go on like that with singleness of purpose, the moment will surely come to all of you when finally a state of great fixation prevails.

'When you hear of this state of absolute unification, you are apt to harbour a feeling of uneasiness mixed with fright, but you must remember that you are by this exercise going to experience the inner realization attained by all the Buddhas because the frontier gate of eternal transmigration is thereby successfully broken down. Some hardships are bound to accompany the attainment.

---

[1] See also p. 119 where similar expressions are quoted. They all point to the abruptness of the Zen experience as advocated by Hui-nêng and his followers.

'As I think of the matter, there have been an innumerable number of the Zen Yogins who have experienced a great joy after going through the state of great fixation and of "great death"; but as to those followers of the Nembutsu who, by means of the Myōgō (*nāmadheya* = "Namu Amida Butsu"), have come even to a fraction of realization, I have heard of only a few of such. It was quite possible for the master of Yeshin In with his virtue, spiritual strength, and sincerity of faith to gain an insight into the truth of Buddhism say in a month or two or at the longest within a year, and find out that he himself was an embodiment of Suchness, if only he could have applied himself to the study of the "*Mu*" or the "three *chin* of flax". It was a great pity that he had to devote himself with wonderful persistency to the recitation of the "Namu Amida Butsu" for forty long years. This is all due to the absence of a great spirit of inquiry even in the most earnest devotee of the Nembutsu. This spirit is surely the highway to final realization.

'Another instance may be seen in the person of Hōnen Shōnin whose morality, humanity, industry, and spiritual virility were phenomenal, and who is said to have been able to read the sūtras in the dark with the light issuing from his own eyes. A soul so highly endowed could easily attain the highest enlightenment if only a spirit of inquiry were present in him. There was no chance indeed for him to complain about the rope being too short to sound the depth of the spring.

'On the other hand, how was it that such masters of great abilities as Yang-ch'i, Huang-lung, Chên-ching, Hsi-kêng, Fo-chien, and Miao-hsi (Tai-hui), who must have known hundreds of thousands of Buddha-names as well as hundreds of thousands of Mantrams or Dhāraṇīs which might be given to their disciples as objects of meditation, should have chosen the "*Mu*" as the means of reaching the goal of an exercise? They would not have done this unless there was something especially recommendable in the "*Mu*". What is this? It is no other than this that the "*Mu*" is apt to awaken a spirit of inquiry in the mind of a Zen Yogin whereas this is difficult with the reciting of the Myōgō—"Namu Amida Butsu".

'The reason, however, why even among Zen followers the Nembutsu or the Shōmyō has been entertained and the rebirth in the Land of Purity desired, is owing to the historical fact that the spirit of Zen was on the wane at the time [that is, in Yüan and especially in Ming], when the Jōdo idea came to be countenanced. While Zen was still in its heyday, not only in China but in India, the masters were strict and strongly conscious of the mission of Zen. Their only fear was that if Zen were allowed to degenerate, its spirit should soon totter to its fall; they never dreamed of referring to the Nembutsu or to the rebirth. But alas, as time went on, there was a lame master towards the end of Ming whose name was Chu-hung of Yün-hsi; his training in Zen was short of finality, his Zen insight did not go deep enough; he found himself wandering about in midway between Nirvāṇa and Saṁsāra. And it was natural for such a soul to abandon the true spirit of Zen discipline and to seek salvation in the echoes of the White Lotus Society, anciently led by Hui-yüan.

'Calling himself the teacher of the Lotus Pond, he wrote commentaries on the sūtras of the Pure Land school to instruct his disciples. Yüan-hsien of Ku-shan, known as Yung-chiao the Teacher, joined forces with Chu-hung by writing a book on the doctrine of the Pure Land (Ch'ing-t'zŭ yao-yü). Since then the purity of the Zen spirit became contaminated beyond repair not only in China itself but in Japan. Even with the master hands of Lin-chi, Tê-shan, Fên-yang, T'zŭ-ming, Huang-lung, Chên-ching, Hsi-kêng, Miao-hsi, and others, it is difficult to push back this tempestuous tide from the field of Zen proper.

'When I say this, I may seem to be unnecessarily hard on the teaching of the Pure Land school and slighting the practice of the Nembutsu. But in truth it is not so. What I blame most is the habit of those Zen followers who, claiming to be training themselves in Zen, are lazy, weak-minded, and while being so slack in the discipline they begin to take fright as they grow older in the thought of an approaching end and start anew with the practice of the Nembutsu, telling people that the Nembutsu is the best method of salvation and most suited for beings of these latter days. They look pious enough, but really they are revilers of Zen, pretending to be its faithful devotees. They are like those insects which, growing from the wooden post, feed upon it and finally tear it down. They deserve therefore a severe criticism.

'Since Ming these Nembutsu followers, disguising themselves to be those of Zen, have been very great in number. They are all worthless muddy-headed students of Zen. I heard, now about fifty years ago, a Zen master complaining of the way things were going on then in the world of Zen: "Alas! What would be the state of affairs three hundred years after this? The whole Zen world might turn into the Nembutsu hall where the wooden bell is heard all the time in accompaniment with the Nembutsu." This is indeed not an unfounded pessimism as far as I can see. Here is the last word of kindness an old man like myself can now offer for your perusal, which is: Do not regard this as a mere form of "*Kwats!*" nor take it for a Dhāraṇī, much less swallow it down as a sort of bitter pill. What is the kindest word of Zen? A monk asked Chao-chou, "Is the dog in possession of the Buddha-nature?" Chou said, "*Mu!*" '[1]

[1] While this was in the press, Mr. Kōson Goto of the Myōshinji monastery, Kyoto, informed me of the existence of a letter of Hakuin, still unpublished, in which he says that 'lately he has come to give the koan of "One Hand" to his students, instead of "*Mu*", because the "One Hand" awakens a spirit of inquiry much more readily than the "*Mu*".' Since then the 'One Hand' has become quite a favourite koan with all the descendants of Hakuin down to this day. The koan is, 'Hear the sound of one hand.' A sound issues when two hands are clapped, and there is no way of its issuing from one single hand. Hakuin now demands his pupils to hear it. One can say that this koan is more intellectual than the '*Mu*'. That Hakuin, who is a great upholder of the inquiring spirit against the mechanical method of the Nembutsu exercise, has now come to use the 'One Hand' as a first eye-opener, is full of signification in the history of Zen consciousness. When I write the history of Zen Buddhism in China, I wish to treat of the subject from a point somewhat different from what has been presented in this Essay.

APPENDICES[1]

I

'Oh, this one rare occurrence,
For which would I not be glad to give ten thousand pieces of
  gold!
A hat is on my head, a bundle around my loins;
And on my staff the refreshing breeze and the full moon I
  carry!'

According to the Second Part of the *Transmission of the
Lamp*,[2] this was given out by the monk Hui-yüan who
came to a realization when he accidentally stumbled while
walking in the courtyard. The same is, however, quoted in
another place as uttered by Chêng-wu Hsiung-yung.

2

Hui-t'ang Tsu-hsin[3] (1025–1100) studied Zen under
Hui-nan of Huang-po for several years, but without
success. One day he was going over the history of Zen, in
which he read this:

A monk came to To-fu and asked, 'How is the bamboo
grove of To-fu?'

---

[1] This section contains some of the 'Tōki-no-ge' (see First Series of *Zen
Essays*, p. 248) uttered by the Zen masters, and the circumstances that
led them to a state of satori, in the hope that they will help students of the
psychology of religion to have a glimpse into the mind of the Zen Yogin,
which is being matured for the final experience. When these are studied
in connection with the technique of the koan exercise, much light will be
shed on the nature of Zen Buddhism.

[2] *Hsü chuan têng lu*, afterwards abbreviated *Hsü-chuan*, consisting of
thirty-six volumes, contains records of the Zen masters between the latter
part of the tenth and the fourteenth centuries. The work is the con-
tinuation of the *Chuan têng lu*. The account of Hui-yüan is found in Vol.
XX, and that of Hsiung-yung in Vol. XIV. Vol. = Fas.

[3] *Hsü-chuan*, XV.

'One or two of the bamboos are slanting.'
'I do not understand.'
'Three or four of them are crooked.'

This 'Mondō' opened Tsu-hsin's eyes. He came up to the master Hui-nan, and when he was about to make bows after spreading out his *tso-chü*, the master smiled and said, 'You have now entered into my room.' Tsu-hsin was very pleased and said, 'If the truth of Zen is such as I have now, why do you make us take up the old stories[1] and exhaust our efforts by striving how to get at their meaning?' Said the master, 'If I did not thus make you strive in every possible way to get at the meaning and make you finally come to a state of non-striving or effortlessness when you see with your own eye and nod to yourself, I am sure you would lose all chance to discover yourself.'

3

'The murmuring mountain stream is the Buddha's broad, long
    tongue;
The mountain itself in its ever-varying hues—is this not his
    Pure Body?
Eighty-four thousand gāthās were recited during the night,
But how may I some day hold them up before others?'

This comes from the pen of Su Tung-po the poet.[2] He was one of the greatest literary stars illuminating the cultural world of Sung. When he was in Ching-nan, he heard of a Zen master called Hao residing at Yü-ch'üan who was noted for his trenchant repartee. Tung-po was also great in this. Wishing to silence the Zen master, one day the poet called on him in disguise. The master asked, 'What is your name?' 'My name is Ch'êng (scale). It scales all the masters of the world.' Hao burst out in a

---

[1] Hua-t'ou is, in short, a Zen interview recorded of the masters. When it is used for training the Zen Yogins, it is a koan.
[2] *Hsü-chuan*, XX.

'*Kwatz!*' and said, 'How much does it weigh?' The conceited poet made no answer; he had to take his hat off to his superior.

4

When I-hai[1] came to Ch'i of Yün-chü, Ch'i asked, 'What is it that thus comes to me?' This opened Hai's mind to a state of satori, and the result was this verse:

' "What's that?" comes from Yün-chü;
Asked thus, one is stupefied:
Even when you nod right away saying, "That's it,"
You cannot yet help being buried alive.'

5

'For twenty years I've pilgrimaged
All the way from east to west:
And now, finding myself at Ch'i-hsien,
Not a step have I ever put forward.'

This comes from Chih-jou,[2] of Ch'i-hsien monastery at Lu-shan, who had a satori under Yüan-t'ung.

6

When Yang-shan was studying Zen under Pai-chang he had such a flowing tongue that to Pai-chang's one word he had ten words to answer. Chang said, 'After me, there will be somebody else who will take care of you.' Yang later went to Wei-shan. Wei asked, 'I am told that while you were under Pai-chang you had ten words to his one;

[1] *Hsü-chuan*, XI.
[2] *Hsü-chuan*, XII.

is that so?' Yang said, 'Yes, that is what they say.' Wei
asked, 'What do you have to state about the ultimate truth
of Buddhism?' Yang was about to open his mouth when the
master shouted '*Kwatz!*' The question was repeated three
times; the mouth vainly opened three times, and the
'*Kwatz!*' was uttered three times. Yang finally broke
down; drooping his head and with tears in his eyes, he said,
'My late master prophesied that I should do better with
someone else, and today I have this very one.'

Determining to experience the truth of Zen in himself,
he spent three years of intense spiritual discipline. One day
Wei-shan saw him sitting under a tree. Approaching, he
touched him on the back with the staff he carried. Yang-
shan turned round, and Wei said, 'O Chi [which was
Yang's name], can you say a word now, or not?' Yang
replied, 'No, not a word, nor would I borrow one from
others.' Wei said, 'O Chi, you understand.'[1]

7

To understand the story of Tao-yüan which is told below,
the knowledge of Pai-chang and his old fox is needed.
Hence the following:

Whenever Pai-chang had his sermon on Zen, there was
an old man in the audience listening to him. One day the
old man did not depart with the rest of the congregation.
Pai-chang then asked him who he was. Answered the old
man: 'At the time of the Buddha Kāśyapa I used to live
in this mountain. One day a monk asked if a Yogin who
went through great spiritual training should be subject to
the law of causation, and I told him, "No, he is not subject
to it."[2] On account of this, I have fallen into the animal
path of existence and have been a fox ever since the time of
the Buddha Kāśyapa. My wish is that you will kindly give
me a statement which will save me from transmigration.'

[1] Quoted by Shih-wu Ch'ing-hung (1272–1352) in his *Sayings*.
[2] *Pu lao yin kuo*, literally, 'not to fall into cause and effect'.

Pai-chang said, 'Then you ask.'

The old man asked, 'Is a Yogin who went through great spiritual training subject to the law of causation, or not?'

Pai-chang replied, 'He does not obscure the law.'[1]

He had scarcely finished when the old man came to an insight as to the working of the law of causation. When leaving Pai-chang, he said: 'I am now freed from the animal path of existence. I used to live at the back of this mountain, and you will be good enough to cremate my body after the funeral rite accorded to a monk.'

Pai-chang made his secretary issue the proclamation that after the midday meal a funeral ceremony for a dead monk would take place and that all the Brotherhood was expected to attend it. The Brotherhood did not know what the proclamation meant, because they knew of no death among them. Pai-chang, however, at the head of the whole party went around to the other side of the mountain, and from a rock-cave he picked out a dead fox. The remains were cremated and, as requested by the strange old man, buried according to the proper rite given to a monk.

This question of *pu lao yin kuo* or *pu mei yin kuo* is a great one not only for Buddhists of all schools but for philosophers and religiously minded people. In other words, it is the question of freedom of the will, it is the question of divine grace, it is the question of transcending karma, it is the question of logic and spirit, of science and religion, of nature and super-nature, of moral discipline and faith. Indeed, it is the most fundamental of all religious questions. If *pu lao yin kuo*, this jeopardizes the whole plan of the universe; for it is *yin-kuo*, the law of causation, that binds existence together, and without the reality of moral responsibility the very basis of society is pulled down.

What then is the difference between *pu-lao* (not falling) and *pu-mei* (not obscuring)? 'Not to fall' is a moral deed, and 'not to obscure' is an intellectual attitude. The former makes one stand altogether outside the realm of causation, which is this world of particulars and where we have our

---

[1] *Pu mei yin kuo*, literally, 'not to obscure cause and effect'.

N

being. This is a contradiction—to be in it and yet to be out of it. In the case of *pu-mei*, 'not to obscure', what happens is the shifting of our mental attitude towards a world above cause and effect. And because of this shifting the whole outlook of life assumes a new tone which may be called spiritual *pu lao yin kuo*.

With this introductory note the following will be intelligible.

Tao-yüan,[1] who was studying Zen under Hui-nan (1002–1069), one day heard two monks engaged in discussion regarding the koan of Pai-chang and the fox. The one said, 'Even when you say *pu mei yin kuo*, this won't make you free from the fox form of existence.' The other immediately responded, 'That is *pu mei yin kuo*, and who had ever fallen into the fox form of existence?' Listening to this, Tao-yüan's inquiring spirit was aroused in an unusual manner, and, without realizing how, he found himself walking up to the mountain; and when he was about to cross the stream, his mind suddenly opened to the truth contained in the koan. As he was later telling the incident to Hui-nan, tears streaked down his cheeks. Nan ordered him to have a rest in his attendant's chair. From a sound sleep he abruptly awoke and uttered this:

> 'Cause and effect—not falling? not obscuring?
> Whether monk or layman, there is nothing for him to shun.
> Here's the man whose sovereign will is peerless,
> Him no bag can hold, no wrappage hide;
> Swinging his staff right and left as he will,
> Straight into a troop of golden-haired lions jumps he, the
> master fox.'

8

I-huai of T'ien-i,[2] who flourished in the latter half of the eleventh century, was the son of a fisherman. Some years

[1] *Hsü-chuan*, XVI.
[2] *Hsü-chuan*, VI.

after he joined the Brotherhood, he came to Ming-chiao to study more of Zen.

Chiao asked, 'What is your name?'

'My name is I-huai.'

'Why don't you have it changed into Huai-i?'

'It was so given to me at the time.'

'Who got the name for you?'

'It is already ten years since I was ordained.'

'How many pairs of sandals did you wear out in your pilgrimage?'

'O master, pray do not crack a joke.'

Chiao asked now: 'I have committed a countless number of errors, so have you. And what say you to this?'

Huai made no reply.

Thereupon Chiao gave him a slap, saying, 'O this idle talker, get out of here!'

When I-huai saw the master another time, the latter said, 'Affirmation obtains not, nor does negation, nor does affirmation-negation; what do you say?'

Huai hesitated, whereupon the master ejected him with a blow. This was repeated four times.

Huai was now made to look after the water supply of the monastery. While he was carrying water, the pole suddenly broke, and the incident gave him the chance to become conscious of the truth hitherto hidden to him. The poem he composed to express the feeling he then had runs as follows:

'One, two, three, four, five, six, seven—
Yes, many thousand feet high is the mountain peak, and lo,
   some one stands there on one leg;
He has carried away the gem from the dragon's jaws,
And Vimalakīrti's[1] secrets he holds in one word.'

Chiao the master, striking his desk confirmed this view.

---

[1] *Hsü-chuan*, V.

9

The monk Ling-t'ao[1] was a disciple of Lê-t'an Huai-têng. When the master asked him what was the idea of the Patriarch, who, coming from the West, is said to have transmitted one single mind-seal, which, pointing directly to the human nature, makes one attain Buddhahood, Ling-t'ao confessed ignorance.

T'an said, 'What were you before you became a monk?'
'I used to be a cowherd.'
'How do you look after the cattle?'
'I go out with them early in the morning and come home when it grows dark.'
'Splendid is your ignorance,' remarked the master.

This remark at once brought Ling-t'ao's mind to a state of satori which was expressed thus:

'Throwing up the tether I am a homeless monk,
The head is shaved, so is the face, and the body wrapped in
    the *chia-sha* (*kāśaya*):
If some one asks, What is the Patriarch's idea of coming
    from the West?
Carrying the staff crosswise I sing out, *La-li-la!*'

10

When Yün-fêng Wên-yüeh[2] came to T'ai-yü Shou-chih for study, he heard the master discoursing to this effect: 'O monks, you are gathered here and consuming so many vegetables each day. But if you call them a mere bunch of vegetables, you go to hell as straight as an arrow flies'; and without further remark, the master left the pulpit. Wên-yüeh was astonished, not knowing what all this meant. In the evening he went up to the master's room, and the master asked, 'What is it that you are seeking?' Yüeh said, 'I am

[1] *Hsü-chuan*, V.
[2] *Hsü-chuan*, IX.

after the truth of the mind.' But the master was not so ready to teach him, for he said: 'Before the wheel of the Dharma (truth) is set moving, the wheel of the staff of life must move. You are yet young and strong; why not go around and beg food for the Brotherhood? My time is all taken up in bearing hunger, and how can I talk of Zen for your sake?' Yüeh meekly obeyed the order and spent his time seeing that the larder of the Brotherhood was properly supplied.

Before long, however, T'ai-yü moved to T'sui-yen and Wên-yüeh followed him. When he asked the master to instruct him in Zen, the master said: 'Buddhism does not mind being covered with too many blisters. For this cold and snowy winter, get a good supply of charcoal for the Brotherhood.' Yüeh obeyed and carried out the master's order faithfully. When he came back, the master again asked him to take up an office in the monastery as there was a vacancy and none was available to fill it. Yüeh did not like this, for he was always ordered about doing things which he thought were not in direct connection with Zen teaching itself; he was sorry to see the master so cross-grained towards him.

While he was working in the back part of the building, perhaps with his mind filled with all sorts of feelings and generally in an intensely strained state of consciousness, the hoops of the wooden cask upon which he was sitting unexpectedly gave way, and he fell from it. This incident was the opportunity to shed an abundance of light into the dark chamber of his hitherto tightly closed mind, and he at once perceived the secret way in which his master's mind had been functioning all the time. He hastily put on his upper robe and came up to see Shou-chih the master. The master greeted him smilingly and said, 'O Wei-na,[1] so pleased to see you realize it!' Twice Yüeh reverentially bowed and went off without a comment.

---

[1] *Karmādāna* in Sanskrit. An office in the Zen monastery, corresponding sometimes to that of master of ceremony, and sometimes to that of general manager or overseer.

II

Yü of Tu-ling,[1] a disciple of Yang-chi (died 1049), used to feed Zen monks on pilgrimage, who passed by his temple. One day he entertained a monk from Yang-chi and asked what his master's teaching of Zen was. The monk said: 'My master would usually ask his pupils the following: A monk once came to Fa-têng and asked, "How should one advance a step when he comes to the end of a pole one hundred feet long?" Fa-têng said, "Oh!"' '

When Yü was told of this, it made him think a great deal. The allusion here is to a stanza by Chang-sha Ching-ch'ên,[2] which runs thus:

'A man immovable at the end of a pole one hundred feet
    long—
He has indeed entered upon the path, but not quite a genuine
    one is he:
Let him yet move forward at the end of a pole one hundred
    feet long,
For then the entire universe extending in the ten quarters is
    his own body.'

The man is already at the end of a pole, and how can he take further steps ahead? But a saltus here is needed to experience the truth of Zen.

One day being invited out, Yü rode on a lame donkey, and when he was crossing over a bridge the donkey got one of its legs caught in a hole, and this at once overthrew the rider on the ground. He loudly exclaimed 'Oh!', and evidently the exclamation waked up his hidden consciousness to a state of satori. The verse gives vent to his experience:

'I have one jewel shining bright,
    Long buried it was underneath worldly worries;
    This morning the dusty veil is off, and restored its lustre,
    Illumining the blue mountains in endless undulations.'[3]

---

[1] *Hsü-chuan*, XIII.
[2] *Transmission of the Lamp*, X.
[3] Quoted also in my *Essays*, Series I, p. 250.

12

The one bright gem discovered by Yü of Tu-ling helped to illumine the mind of Shou-tuan of Pai-yün.[1] Yang-chi who was also his master one day asked him who ordained him as a Zen monk. Tuan answered, 'Yü of Tu-ling.' Whereupon Chi said: 'I understand that Yü had a fall from a lame donkey, which led him to satori. Do you know by heart the verse he then composed?' Tuan proceeded to recite the whole verse beginning with 'I have one jewel shining bright. . . .'

When he finished the whole verse, Yang-chi gave a hearty laugh and quickly left his seat.

Shou-tuan was astonished, and no sleep had he that night. With the first blush of the day he appeared before the master and inquired of him what was the meaning of his laugh. It happened to be the end of the year. So asked the master, 'Did you see yesterday those devil-chasers going about in the streets?'

'Yes, master,' Tuan replied.

'Compared with them you are somewhat at a disadvantage, are you not?'

This remark was another case of astonishment on the part of Shou-tuan, who asked: 'What does that mean, master? Pray tell me.'

Chi said, 'They love to be laughed at whereas you are afraid of being laughed at.'

Tuan got his satori.

13

Tsu-yin Chü-nê[2] of Shu district, who flourished in the middle part of the eleventh century, was a great scholar versed in the *Puṇḍarīka* and other schools of Buddhist

[1] *Hsü-chuan*, XIII.
[2] *Hsü-chuan*, XIII.

philosophy, and even elderly scholars were willing to study under him. Evidently he did not know anything of Zen. One day he had a caller who was acquainted with the doings of Zen in the South. He said that the entire Buddhist world of China was then taken up by the teaching of Bodhidharma, and that Ma-tsu, one of his ablest descendants, who appeared to fulfil the prophecy of Prajñātala, had exercised great influence over the Buddhist scholars of the country, so that even men of learning and understanding who were renowned throughout the province of Shu, such as Liang and Chien, either gave up their own pupils or burned their library of the commentaries, in order to master the teaching of Zen.

Chü-nê was very much impressed with the report of his Zen friend. Advised strongly by him to go out into the world and see the state of affairs by himself, Chü-nê left his native province and wandered about some years in Ching and Ch'u but without seeing any result. He then moved further west and stayed in Hsiang-chou for ten years under Yung of Tung-shan. One day he was reading a treatise on the *Avataṁsaka* and was deeply impressed by the following passage, which opened finally his mind to the truth of Zen:

'Mount Sumeru towers in the great ocean attaining the altitude of 84,000 yojanas, and its summit is not to be scaled by means of hands and legs. This illustrates that the mountain of 84,000 human woes is rising from the great ocean of passions. When beings attain the state of consciousness in which they cherish no thoughts [of relativity] and from which all strivings vanish, even when confronting this world of multiplicities, their passions will naturally be drained off. All the worldly woes now turn into the mountain of all-knowledge and the passions into the ocean of all-knowledge. On the contrary, when the mind is filled with thoughts and reflections of relativity, there are attachments. Then the greater grow worldly woes and the deeper the passions, and a man is barred from reaching the summit of knowledge which makes up the essence of Buddhahood.'

Chü-nê then observed: 'According to Shih-kuang, "Not

a cue to get hold of," and according to Ma-tsu, "Ignorance since the beginningless past has melted away today." These are indeed no lies!'

14

Ch'ing-yüan Fo-yen of Lung-mên[1] who died in 1120 was first a student of the Vinaya; later, reading the *Puṇḍarīka* he came across the passage, 'This Dharma is something that goes beyond the realm of thought and discrimination.' This impressed him, so he came to his teacher and asked what was this Dharma transcending intelligence. The teacher failed to enlighten him, who then saw that mere learning and scholarship could not solve the ultimate problem of this existence subject to birth and death.

Fo-yen now travelled south in order to see Fa-yen of Tai-p'ing. While begging through the county of Lu, he stumbled and fell on the ground. While suffering pain, he overheard two men railing at each other, when a third one who interceded remarked, 'So I see the passions still cherished by both of you.' He then had a kind of satori.

But to whatever questions he asked of Fa-yen, the answer was, 'I cannot surpass you; the thing is to understand all by yourself.' Sometimes Yen said, 'I do not understand myself, and I cannot surpass you.' This kind of remark incited Ch'ing-yüan's desire all the more to know Zen. He decided to get the matter settled by his senior monk Yüan-li, but Li pulled him by the ear and going around the fire-place kept on saying, 'The best thing is to understand all by yourself.' Ch'ing-yüan insisted: 'If there is really such a thing as Zen, why not uncover the secret for me? Otherwise, I shall say it is all a trick.' Li, however, told him: 'Some day you will come to realize all that has been going on today between you and me.'

When Fa-yen moved away from Tai-p'ing, Ch'ing-yüan left him, and spent the summer at Ching-shan,

---

[1] *Hsü-chuan*, XXV.

where he got very well acquainted with Ling-yüan. Ch'ing-yüan now asked his advice, saying, 'Lately, I have come to know of a master in the city whose sayings seem to suit my intelligence much better.' But Ling-yüan persuaded him to go to Fa-yen who was the best of the Zen masters of the day, adding that those whose words he seemed to understand best were merely teachers of philosophy and not real Zen masters.

Ch'ing-yüan followed his friend's advice, and came back to his former master. One cold night he was sitting alone and tried to clear away the ashes in the fire-place to see if there were any piece of live charcoal left. One tiny piece as large as a pea happened to be discovered way down in the ashes. He then reflected that the truth of Zen would also reveal itself as one dug down to the rock-bed of consciousness. He took up the history of Zen known as the *Transmission of the Lamp* from his desk, and his eye fell upon the story of the P'o-tsao-to ('broken range'),[1] which unexpectedly opened his mind to a state of satori. The following is the stanza he then composed extempore:

'The birds are too-tooing in the woods,
With the garment covered up I sit alone all night.
A tiny piece of live charcoal deeply buried in the ashes tells
    the secret of life:
The cooking range is broken to pieces when the spirit knows
    where to return.
Revealed everywhere shines the truth, but men see it not,
    confused is the mind;
Simple though the melody is, who can appreciate it?
Thinking of it, long will its memory abide with me;
Wide open is the gate, but how lonely the scene!'

The story of the P'o-tsao-to alluded to in the text is as follows: The P'o-tsao-to is the name given by Hui-an to one of his disciples at Sung-yüeh. It literally means, 'a broken range fallen to pieces', which illustrates an incident in the life of a nameless Zen master, whereby he became

---

[1] For the story, see below.

notorious. There was a shrine in one of the Sung-yüeh villages where a lonely range was kept. This was the object of worship for the country people far and near, who here roasted alive many victims for sacrifice.

The nameless one one day appeared in the shrine accompanied by his attendants. He struck the range three times with his staff, and said: 'Tut! O you an old range, are you not a mere composite of brick and clay? Whence your holiness? Whence your spirituality? And yet you demand so many victims roasted alive for sacrifice!' So saying, the master struck the range for another three times. The range then tipped by itself, and falling on the ground broke in pieces.

After a while there suddenly appeared a man in blue dress with a high headgear, and approaching the master bowed reverentially to him. The master asked who he was, and he answered: 'I am the spirit of the range enshrined here. I have been here for a long time owing to my previous karma. But listening to your sermon on the doctrine of no-birth, I am now released from the bondage and born in the heavens. To offer my special thanks to you I have come.' Said the master: 'No-birth is the original nature of your being. No sermonizing of mine was needed.' The heavenly being bowed again and vanished.

Later on the attendant-monks and others asked the master: 'We have been with you for ever so long, but we have never been permitted to listen to your personal discourses on the Dharma. What effective teaching did the range-spirit get from you which enabled him to be born immediately in the heavens?'

The master said, 'What I told him was simply that he was a composite of brick and clay; I had no further teaching specially meant for him.'

The attendant-monks and others stood quietly without saying a word.

The master remarked, 'Do you understand?'

The chief secretary of the monastery said, 'No, we do not.'

The master continued, 'The original nature of all beings
—why do you not understand it?'

The monks all made bows to the master, whereupon
exclaimed the master: 'It's fallen, it's fallen! It's broken to
pieces, it's broken to pieces!'[1]

15

Wên-chun of Lê-t'an (1061–1115)[2] devoted himself
while young to the mastery of Buddhist philosophy but
later abandoned it, saying that he did not care very much
for it. He then began to study Zen, and going south stayed
with Chên-ju of Wei-shan for many years. However, he
made no progress. He came to Chên-ching of Chiu-fêng,
who was another great Zen master of the time.

Ching asked, 'Where is your native town?'

'Hsing-yüan Fu.'

'Where do you come from now?'

'Tai-yang.'

'Where did you pass your summer?'

'At Wei-shan.'

Ching now produced his hand, saying, 'How is it that my
hand so resembles the Buddha's?'

Chun was dumbfounded and unable to make any
answer.

Ching scolded: 'So far you have been fluent enough in
answering all my questions naturally and in a most splendid
manner. As soon as the subject turned to the Buddha's
hand, you halt. Where is the trouble?'

Chun confessed ignorance.

Ching said, 'Everything lies open in full revelation right
before you; and whom would you get to teach you?'

For ten years Chun stayed with his master Chên-ching
and went about wherever he moved. Ching was a silent
teacher and gave out no special instruction to anybody

[1] *Transmission of the Lamp*, IV.
[2] *Hsü-chuan*, XXII.

although his pupils grew considerably in number. When a monk entered his room for advice he would close his eyes and sit up on his knees and say nothing. If he saw somebody coming to him, he would rise, go out into the garden, and join the gardeners in hoeing. This was his usual way of dealing with his disciples. Wên-chun used to say to his friend Kung: 'Has the master no intention whatever to teach his followers in the Dharma? It is hard to know him.'

One day Wên-chun removed the dam with a stick, and while washing his clothes his mind suddenly woke to a state of satori. He ran to the master and reported to him all that happened to him. But the master coldly blamed him, saying, 'Why have you to be so unmannerly in this?'

16

K'ê-ch'in Fo-kuo[1] who died in A.D. 1135 was born in a Confucian family. While young, he was a great devourer of the classics. One day he went to a Buddhist monastery where he happened to read Buddhist books, and felt as if he were recalling his old memories. 'I must have been a monk in my previous life,' he thought.

Later he was ordained as a Buddhist priest, and devoted himself diligently to the mastery of Buddhist philosophy. He fell ill and when almost at the point of death he reflected: 'The right way to the attainment of Nirvāṇa as taught by the Buddhas is not to be found in words and mere ratiocination. I have been seeking it in sounds and forms and no doubt I deserve death.' When he recovered, he quitted his old method, and came to a Zen master called Chên-chüeh Shêng. Shêng's instruction consisted in making his own arm bleed by sticking a knife into it and remarking that each drop of the blood came from T'sao-ch'i. T'sao-ch'i is where Hui-nêng, the sixth patriarch of

---

[1] *Hsü-chuan*, XXV. He is best known as the author of the *Pi-yen-lu*. His honorary title is 'Yüan-wu Ch'an-shih' (Zen master of Perfect Enlightenment).

Chinese Zen, founded his school, and the remark meant that Zen demanded one's life for its mastery.

Thus inspired, Fo-kuo visited many Zen masters. They were all very well impressed with his attainment, and some even thought that it was he who would establish a new original school in the teaching of Rinzai (Lin-chi). Finally, Kuo came to Fa-yen of Wu-tsu monastery, who, however, refused to confirm Kuo's view of Zen. Kuo thought Fay-en was deliberately contradicting him. Giving vent to his dissatisfaction in some disrespectful terms, Kuo was about to leave Fa-yen, who simply said, 'Wait until you become seriously ill one day when you will have to remember me.'

While at Chin-shan, Fo-kuo contracted a fever from which he suffered terribly. He tried to cope with it with all his Zen experiences heretofore attained, but to no purpose whatever. He then remembered Fa-yen's prophetic admonition. As soon as he felt better, therefore, he went back to the Wu-tsu monastery. Fa-yen was pleased to have his repentant pupil back. Before long Yen had a visitor whose official business being over was to go back to the capital. Being asked by him as to the teaching of Zen, Fa-yen said: 'Do you know a romantic poem whose last two lines somewhat reminds us of Zen? The lines run:

'For the maid she calls—why so often, when there's no special work to do?
Only this—perchance her voice is overheard by her lover.'

When this was recited, the young officer said, 'Yes, yes, master.' But he was told not to take it too easily.

Fo-kuo heard of this interview when he came back from outside, and asked: 'I am told you recited the romantic poem for the young visitor while I was away. Did he understand?'

Fa-yen replied, 'He recognizes the voice.'

Fo-kuo said, 'As long as the line says, "The thing is to have the lover overhear her voice", and if the officer heard this voice, what is wrong with him?'

Without directly answering the question, the master abruptly said: 'What is the Patriarch's idea of coming from the West? The cypress-tree in the court-yard. How is this?' This at once opened Fo-kuo's eye to the truth of Zen. He rushed out of the room when he happened to see a cock on the railing give a cry, fluttering its wings. He said, 'Is this not the voice?' The verse he then composed was:[1]

'The golden duck behind the brocade screens has ceased
    sending out its odorous smoke;
Amidst flute playing and singing, he retired, thoroughly in
    liquor and supported by others:
The happy event in the life of a romantic youth,
It is his sweetheart alone that is allowed to know.'

To this Fa-yen the master added: 'The great affair of life that has caused the Buddhas and patriarchs to appear among us is not meant for small characters and inferior vessels. I am glad that I have been a help to your delight.'

17

Hui-ch'in Fo-chien[2] of Tai-ping studied Zen for many years under different masters and thought he was fully accomplished in it. But Fa-yen of Wu-tsu Shan refused to sanction his view, which offended him greatly. He left the master, as did his friend Fo-kuo. But the latter returned to Wu-tsu and attained full realization under him. Fo-chien also came back after a while, but his real intention was to go somewhere else. Fo-kuo, however, advised him to stay with the master, saying, 'We have been separated from each other more than a month, but what do you think of me now since I saw you last?' 'This is what puzzles me,' was his reply.

The signification of this conversation is that Fo-kuo,

[1] This was already cited in the First Series, p. 249.
[2] *Hsü-chuan*, XXV.

as was already recorded under him, had his satori soon after he came back to his former master. This fact, occurring during the month's separation from his friend, had caused such a change in Kuo's spiritual life that Chien wondered what was the cause and meaning of this transformation.

Fo-chien decided to stay at Wu-tsu Shan with his old master Fa-yen and his good friend Fo-kuo. One day Fa-yen referred to the 'mondō' between Chao-chou and a monk:

'The monk asked, "What is your way of teaching?"

'Chao-chou said, "I am deaf; speak louder, please."

'The monk repeated the question.

'Then Chao-chou said, "You ask me about my way of teaching, and I have already found out yours." '

This 'mondō' served to open Fo-chien's mind to satori. He now asked the master, 'Pray point out for me what is the ultimate truth of Zen.' The master answered, 'A world of multiplicities is all stamped with the One.' Chien bowed and retired.

Later when Fo-kuo and Fo-chien were talking on Zen, mention was made of Tung-szŭ's asking Yang-shan about the bright gem from the sea of Chen.[1] When the talk turned to 'no reasoning to advance', Fo-kuo demanded, 'When it is said that the gem is already in hand, why this statement again that there are no words for reply, nor is there any reasoning to advance?' Fo-chien did not know what reply to make. On the following day, however, he

---

[1] The story of the gem is this: Yang-shan came to Hui of Tung-szŭ (A.D. 742–823) for a Zen interview. Hui asked, 'Where is your native place?'

'I come from Kuang-nan.'

'I am told that there is a bright-shining gem in the sea of Chên, of Kuang-nan; is this right?'

'Yes, that's right.'

'What is the shape of the gem?'

'While the moon is shining, it is revealed.'

'Did you bring it along?'

'Yes, I did.'

'Why do you not get it out for your old master?'

'I saw Wei-shan yesterday, and he also wanted to see the gem; but there were no words in which to frame my reply, nor was there any reasoning I could advance.'

said, 'Tung-szŭ wanted the gem and nothing else, but what Yang-shan produced was just an old wicker work.' Fo-kuo confirmed the view, but told him to go and see the master personally.

One day when Fo-chien came to the master's room and was at the point of addressing him, the master rebuked him terribly. Poor Chien had to retire in a most awkward manner. Back in his own quarters, he shut himself up in the room while his heart was in rebellion against the master.

Fo-kuo found this out quietly, and came to his friend's room and knocked at the door. Chien called out, 'Who is it?' Finding that it was his dear friend Kuo, he told Kuo to come in. Kuo innocently asked: 'Did you see the master? How was the interview?' Chien now reproached him saying: 'It was according to your advice that I have stayed here, and what is the outcome of the trick? I have been terribly rebuked by that old master of ours.' Kuo burst out into a hearty laugh and said, 'Do you remember what you told me the other day?' 'What do you mean?' retorted the discontented Chien. Kuo then added, 'Did you say that while Tung-szŭ wanted the gem and nothing else, what Yang-shan produced was just an old wicker work?'

When his own statement was repeated now by his friend, Chien at once saw the point. Thereupon both Kuo and Chien called on the master, who, seeing them approach, abruptly remarked, 'O Brother Ch'ien, this time you surely have it!'

18

Fo-têng Shou-hsün (1079–1134)[1] began to study Zen under Kuang-chien Ying. He came later to Tai-p'ing, where Fo-chien resided, but was at a loss how to take hold of Zen. He put a seal on his bedding and made this vow: 'If I do not attain the experience of Zen in this life, this will never be spread to rest my body in.' He sat in meditation

---

[1] *Hsü-chuan*, XXIX.

during the day, but the night was passed standing up. He applied himself to the mastery of Zen most assiduously as if he had lost his parents. Seven weeks thus elapsed, when Fo-chien gave a sermon saying, 'A world of multiplicities is all stamped with the One.' This opened the eye of Shou-hsün. Fo-chien said, 'What a pity that the lustrous gem has been carried away by this lunatic!'

He then said to Hsün: 'According to Ling-yün, "Since I once saw the peach bloom, I have never again cherished a doubt." What is this when no doubts are ever cherished by anybody?'

Hsün answered, 'Don't say that Ling-yün never cherishes a doubt; it is in fact impossible for any doubt to be cherished anywhere even now.'

Chien said: 'Hsüan-sha criticized Ling-yün, saying, "You are all right as far as you go, but you have not yet really penetrated." Now tell me where is this unpenetrated spot.'

Hsün replied, 'Most deeply I appreciate your grand-motherly kindness.'

Chien gave his approval to this remark. Thereupon, Hsün produced the following stanza:

'All day he has been looking at the sky yet without lifting his
    head,
Seeing the peach in full bloom he has for the first time raised
    his eyebrows:
Mind you, however, there's still a world-enveloping net;
Only when the last barrier-gate is broken through, there is
    complete rest.'

Yüan-wu Fo-kuo who heard of this had some misgiving about Shou-hsün's attainment. He thought he would give it a test and see for himself how genuine Hsün was. He called him in and had a walk with him in the mountain. When they came to a deep pool, Kuo rudely pushed his companion into the water. No sooner he did this than he asked:

'How about Niu-t'ou before he saw the Fourth Patriarch?'[1]

'Deep is the pool, many are the fish.'

'How afterwards?'

'The high tree invites a breeze.'

'How when he is seen and not seen?'

'The legs stretched are the legs bent.'

The test fully satisfied Fo-kuo, who was by the way Shou-hsün's uncle in faith.

---

[1] For the interview of Niu-t'ou and Tao-hsin (the fourth patriarch of Zen in China), see my *Essays*, First Series, pp. 201–202. This interview has frequently been made a subject of Zen 'mondō'.